Christmas in
SCOTLAND

Winter reflections in Loch Lomond, near Glasgow

Christmas in
SCOTLAND

Christmas Around the World
From World Book

World Book, Inc.

a Scott Fetzer company

CHICAGO

STAFF

President
Robert C. Martin

EDITORIAL

Managing Editor
Maureen Mostyn Liebenson

Associate Editor
Shawn Brennan

Writer
Ellen Hughes

Manager, Cartographic Database
Wayne K. Pichler

Permissions Editor
Janet T. Peterson

Director, Product Development
and Research Services
Paul Kobasa

Head, Indexing Services
David Pofelski

Staff Indexer
Tina Trettin

ART

Executive Director
Roberta Dimmer

Art Director
Wilma Stevens

Senior Designer
Brenda B. Tropinski

Senior Photographs Editor
Sandra Dyrlund

Photographs Editor
Carol Parden

PRODUCT PRODUCTION

Manufacturing Manager
Barbara Podczerwinski

Manufacturing Assistant Manager
Valerie Piarowski

Senior Production Manager
Madelyn Underwood

Print Promotional Manager
Marco Morales

Proofreaders
Anne Dillon
Chad Rubel

Text Processing
Gwendolyn Johnson

World Book wishes to thank the following individuals for their contributions to CHRISTMAS IN SCOTLAND:
Irene Keller, Nancy Moroney, Katie Sharp, Howard Timms, and Lerwick Up Helly Aa Committee, Shetland.

World Book, Inc.
233 N. Michigan Avenue
Chicago, IL 60601

For information on other World Book publications, call
1-800-WORLDBK (967-5325). For information about sales to schools and libraries, call 1-800-975-3250 (United States) or 1-800-837-5365 (Canada).

Printed in the United States of America by The HF Group LLC, North Manchester, Indiana
8th printing April 2014

Library of Congress Cataloging-in-Publication Data
Christmas in Scotland : Christmas around the world / from World Book.
   p. cm.
   Includes index.
   Summary: Describes the celebration of Christmas in Scotland, both in the past and in the present, and includes crafts, carols, and recipes.
   ISBN 0-7166-0860-X
   1. Christmas—Scotland—Juvenile literature. 2. Scotland—Social life and customs—Juvenile literature. [1. Christmas—Scotland. 2. Scotland—Social life and customs.] I. World Book.
GT4987.45.C57 2001
394.2663'09411—dc21
                                    2001026838

CONTENTS

The Scottish Spirit of the Season 6

Ancient People, Ancient Celebrations. 12

Christmas in Scotland: Then and Now 21

Hogmanays of Auld 34

Hogmanay and Ne'er's Day Today 45

Holidays on the Scottish Islands. 54

Scottish Crafts 65

Scottish Carols 71

Scottish Recipes 73

Glossary 77

Index. 78

Acknowledgments 80

THE SCOTTISH SPIRIT OF THE SEASON

In Scotland, the holidays are a time to come together with family and friends. Holiday bonfires light the night across the Scottish Highlands, on the North Sea islands, in Edinburgh, and in other cities and villages, while all-night parties warm nearly every home.

Even during the centuries when the public celebration of Christmas was banned in Scotland, the spirit of the season survived. Some Scottish people kept Christmas in their homes and hearts—while shifting focus of the season to the party on New Year's Eve. In Scotland, that grand party is called *Hogmanay.*

Once just a single day when children called at friends' houses for oatmeal cakes and presents, Hogmanay is now a five-day festival drawing people from all over the world to Edinburgh, Scotland's capital and longtime center of Hogmanay celebration. In recent years, the wild and merry atmosphere of Hogmanay has reached Mardi Gras-like proportions as some 200,000 people crowd Edinburgh's city center to ring in the New Year Scottish-style.

The Scots may not have invented the New Year's Eve celebration, but they have certainly made it their own. And though it got its name by the end of the 17th century, the

George Square in Glasgow lights up during the Christmas season.

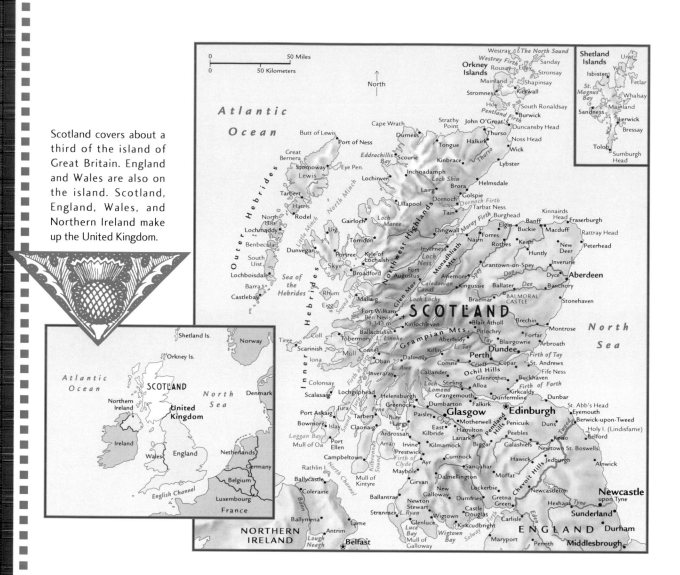

Scotland covers about a third of the island of Great Britain. England and Wales are also on the island. Scotland, England, Wales, and Northern Ireland make up the United Kingdom.

roots of Hogmanay are firmly embedded in the ancient rites and rituals, the turbulent history, and the enduring spirit of the people of Scotland.

A RICH ANCESTRY

Historians believe that the first people to live in Scotland came from other parts of Britain or the European mainland more than 7,000 years ago. About 1800 B.C., people called the *Beaker folk* settled in Northern Scotland. Their name comes from small clay containers

called *beakers*, which they buried with their dead. Celtic tribes probably had migrated to Scotland by the 600's B.C. The Celts came from western Europe.

A Roman army commanded by Gnaeus Julius Agricola, the Roman governor of England, invaded Scotland in A.D. 80. The Romans called Scotland *Caledonia*. The invaders called the people of Scotland *Picts* (painted people) because they painted or tattooed their bodies.

Agricola defeated the Picts and returned to Rome. The Romans who remained in Scotland had trouble controlling the Picts. The Pictish tribes fought the Romans for many years. The Romans built forts and walls to keep the Picts out of the province of Britain. The Romans left in the early 400's. Later, the Picts fought the Teutonic conquerors of Britain, the Angles and the Saxons. The Picts disappeared as a people about A.D. 900.

About A.D. 500, a Celtic tribe called the *Scots* came from northern Ireland and settled on Scotland's west coast. Saint Columba, an Irish monk, followed the Scots in 563. He founded a monastery and, with the help of the Scots, began to convert the Picts to Christianity.

In A.D. 843, Kenneth MacAlpin, king of the Scots, became king of the Picts as well. He established Alba, the first united kingdom in Scotland.

RELIGIOUS REFORM AND THE STRUGGLE FOR INDEPENDENCE

In the late 900's, many violent struggles for control of Scotland began. The English wanted to control the entire island of Great Britain, but the Scottish people wanted to keep their independence. From the late 1200's until the late 1600's, Scotland was sometimes independent and sometimes ruled by England. Finally, English and Scottish leaders decided that their countries must be united to keep peace. In 1707, they passed the Act of Union, which joined Scotland, England, and Wales into one kingdom.

The Roman Catholic Church was the official church of Scotland until the 1560's, when John Knox, a Scottish minister, led the Scots in establishing a reformed Protestant national church. During the late 16th century, the Reformation—the religious movement that led to Protestantism in Europe—overturned many religious beliefs and brought a stricter regimen for living to Scotland. The reformed church considered the keeping of Christmas to be papish (Roman Catholic) and pagan. By 1651, Christmas celebration was banned throughout Great Britain.

But you can't deprive the Scottish of a good time, and so they continued to celebrate Christmas in secret. Slowly the holiday turned from a religious to a secular festival. By the 17th century, the unique Scottish holiday became known as Hogmanay.

A DISTINCTIVE HOLIDAY STYLE

The Scottish national emblem is the prickly thistle and its national motto, *Nemo Me Impune Lacessit!*, which translates, "No one bothers me without being hurt!" Scotland treasures its unique nature as a country and mightily resists any softening or blurring of its cherished traditions.

Scotland's long history of ancestors, invaders, political struggles, and religious strife have resulted in a distinctive holiday style. And nowhere is this style more evident than in the celebration of Hogmanay—the holiday the Scottish are proud to call their own.

Scotland's flag (top) is called *St. Andrew's Cross.* The flag has never been officially adopted but the Scottish people have flown it for hundreds of years. Scotland's version of the Royal British Arms (above) includes the arms of Scotland, England, and Ireland. At the bottom of the coat of arms is the Scottish national motto, *Nemo Me Impune Lacessit!*, which translates, "No one bothers me without being hurt!"

LANG MAY YOUR LUM REEK

The Hogmanay toast "Lang may your lum reek"—which translates "Long may smoke rise from your chimney"—is a wish for long life and prosperity.

Scots take their toasts seriously, especially at Hogmanay. Some are sung for verse after verse, others come straight to the point.

In Scotland today, many a glass is raised to one of these old favorites at Hogmanay:

Weel may we a' be,
Ill may we never see,
Here's to the King
And guid companie!

or:

And let us wish that ane an' a'
Our friends baith far and near
May aye (always) enjoy in
*   times to come*
A hearty guid new year.

or:

Happy New Year t' ye;
God send ye plenty.
Where ye have one pound note,
I wish ye may have twenty.

or:

Here's to all those that I love.
Here's to all those that love me.
And here's to all those that love
*   those that I love,*
And all those that love those
*   that love me.*

The most common Scottish New Year's toast?

A guid New Year to ane an' a',
And monie may ye see.
*   (A good New Year to one*
and all, and many may you
see.)

Finally, there's the rousing:

Here's tae (to) us. Wha's
(who's) like us.

With the proud reply:

Damn few, and they're a' deid.

Well-wishing Hogmanay toasts hit straight to the spirit of the occasion. The old year is passing, and the year ahead is filled with possibility. Everyone is focused on making a clean break with the past and getting a fresh start in the new year.

In Scotland, on New Year's Eve and also on New Year's Day, fortunetelling tools are all around you—from the coins in your pocket and the animals in the field to the cheese on the table and the water in the well.

OFF TO A GOOD START

- Place a silver coin on your doorstep before you retire on New Year's Eve. If the coin is still there in the morning—or better yet, has multiplied in the night—you are in for a good year. If the coin is gone, you're off to a bad start, financially.
- Look through a hole in a round of cheese. You may see your future mate.
- Check the ashes from the fire on New Year's morning. Is there anything like a footprint there? If it appears headed in toward the fire, someone will be added to your family this year. If it looks headed out toward the door, someone may be removed before the year is finished.

Checking for footprints, because of their possibly powerful message, was sometimes taken to extremes in the past. People would even climb onto the roof to look down the "lum" for any warning footprint smudges headed out the chimney.

Then, there are ways to give fortune a positive push:

- Be the first to rise on New Year's Day. Be first in your house, and first in your neighborhood for extra good luck.
- When you get up, wear something new on the first day of the new year. If a baby born on this day gives three cries, he or she will have a long and happy life.
- To get everything off on the right foot this year, do a token amount of every kind of work you would do throughout the year this day. While all real work is stopped for the day, making a little start in anything will help it go well all year long.
- Burn up the bad of the past. In the old ceremonial burning of *Cailleach*, or the spirit of Old Winter, families would select a special piece of wood, then carve the face of an old woman on it. Sometimes, the Cailleach would even be given a person's name. Everyone would gather to watch this Cailleach be consumed by a roaring fire. All the bad luck and disagreements of the past year were thought to burn up with it.
- Be sure to cream the well first thing on New Year's morning.

This is a very old, but very well-known Scottish New Year's custom. The first person to draw water from the well on the first day of the year is said to "get the cream" of the well, or get the very best water the well has to offer. Young women thought the water would bring them luck in love, and so wanted the first sip. Scottish farmers thought this water helped bring a good supply of milk and butter in the coming year. Therefore, cows would be given some of it to drink.

KEEP THE HOME FIRES BURNING

According to Scottish tradition, the state of the house on New Year's Day predicts its well-being during the year ahead. Empty pockets or empty cupboards this day mean a year of poverty ahead.

A fire is kept blazing in the hearth all day, burning as a symbol of warmth and prosperity for the year to come. It is important that the fire blaze, not smolder, for a smoldering fire means adversity. Also, any piece of peat or coal which rolled away from the fire could signal a person leaving the home during the year to come.

Fire cannot be shared this day. Should a neighbor ask for kindling or embers to start a fire in their own cold cottage today, the request would be denied. No friend would ask for an ember from your fire on New Year's Day because even to make such a request

is to wish bad luck on the family. Taking fire away amounts to trying to steal a home's good fortune.

Nothing should go out of the house on the first day of the year before something comes in. A guest must arrive with a present, no matter how small, to keep the balance for the house.

An old Scottish woman told a story about going to the store on New Year's Day when she was a girl. Working as a servant, she was washing clothes on New Year's morning and ran out of soap. She went to the store without money and asked the shopkeeper to give her some soap, saying her mistress would pay when she returned.

The shopkeeper refused, saying "If naething's brocht in, naething's ge'en out." Then, she told the girl to go outside and bring in a single blade of grass.

When the girl brought in the grass, the shopkeeper was happy to give the girl the soap and wait for payment later. Something had to come in before anything went out. The blade of grass was an excellent choice. Grass was free, easy to find, and, like water and fire, is a symbol of good luck on New Year's Day.

Borrowing on New Year's Day also is discouraged. Letting anything go out of the house was thought to take your luck for the year with it. A person wouldn't even throw out trash today.

A marriage should not be proposed in one year and carried out in the next. "Straddling" the two years is bad luck for the new couple. Also, a dead body should not remain in the house on New Year's Day. If a family member died at the end of the year, the services would be hurried to meet the year-end deadline.

Toasting, as shown in this 1872 drawing, is an important ancient Scottish tradition, especially at Hogmanay.

ANCIENT PEOPLE, ANCIENT CELEBRATIONS

Since ancient times, the darkest nights of winter in Scotland have burned bright with celebration. For centuries, magical Druid, Celtic, and Viking fire festivals filled the days and nights surrounding the winter solstice and the beginning of a new year.

Since prehistoric times, people have depended on the sun for survival and worshiped it as a god. It was the source of light, warmth, food, fire, and life. It nourished their land and enriched their harvest.

Each autumn, they watched the sun god move away—its power, light, and warmth weakening. The days became shorter and darker. Then just as they began to fear the sun god would go away forever, it slowly started to return, bringing with it the warmth, light, and ripening of spring: the winter solstice.

THE BIRTHDAY OF THE UNCONQUERED SUN

The annual return of the sun god was celebrated with feasting and drinking. Special rites were held and sacrifices

Dusk over frozen Linlithgow
Loch near Linlithgow Palace

Burning of the Clavie in Burghead, Elgin, on New Year, 1875

were offered to please the sun god. After the days of the sun worshipers, the Romans held their own midwinter celebration, the Saturnalia, which lasted from mid-December until December 24th. This celebration was the precedent for midwinter festivals to come in Scotland and all across Europe. The focus of the celebration was a day called *Dies Natalis Solis Invicta*, the "Birthday of the Unconquered Sun."

Long after pagan worship ceased and Christianity spread across Europe, this special day continued to be the focus of the midwinter celebration. Christian leaders adapted the estab-lished old pagan customs into their religion, and gave them a Christian spin. The "Birthday of the Unconquered Sun" became a celebration of the birthday of Jesus Christ. The new Christian holiday with the ancient pagan roots became a potpourri of praying and partying.

FIRE AND FEASTING

During their five-century invasion of Scotland's coasts, the Vikings made their mark in many ways. They also brought their own midwinter festival to Scotland. They called it *Yule*, a name by which the holiday season is still known today. Their hearty Yule celebration comprised 24 days of partying, beginning with a massive feast on the eve of Yule. That evening they toasted their sun goddess, Freya, with large quantities of liquor, after which they went out to light the winter night with a great bonfire in Freya's honor.

To this day, fire festivals are a big part of Yule celebrations all over Scotland: from the big bonfire in Biggar to Stonehaven's fireball parade; from Burghead's "Burning of the Clavie" and Comrie's Flambeaux torch procession to the burning of a Viking galley during the Shetlands' Norse celebration, Up-Helly-A'.

In addition to these, there were many other ancient Celtic, Druid, Viking, and Roman superstitions, traditions, and rites. They still cling to Scotland's holiday celebrations today.

ANCIENT GREENERY

Evergreens like holly, mistletoe, rowan (a European ash with a red, berrylike fruit), and juniper—representing life and hope, and imbued with a wealth of ancient religious and superstitious meanings—have been used to decorate Scottish homes during midwinter solstice for centuries before Christmas itself arrived.

Holly has been part of the Scottish midwinter celebration for more than 2,000 years, and it was important in Roman and Druid winter solstice festivals. A plant that grows green and robust during the darkest days of winter, holly once was used to honor the Ro-

man god of fertility and planting, Saturn, during his winter solstice festival, Saturnalia.

A Scottish pagan ritual called for placing holly in every part of the home in winter. Holly leaves, it was thought, provided shelter to the little fairies of the forest. Bringing the holly inside was a way to invite the tiny folk to share the comfort of your home's warmth and bring good fortune to you in return.

The Druid culture revered holly as an evergreen that kept the world beautiful when all other plants had shed their leaves and turned brown. The Druids also believed that red holly berries contained the blood of a goddess.

Druids, and other ancient cultures, believed holly provided protection. Some Druids would stick defensive sprigs of holly in their hair whenever

Holly has been part of the Scottish midwinter celebration for more than 2,000 years.

they ventured into the forest. Others would trim their doors and windows with holly to ward off or trap any evil spirits trying to enter a house during the holiday season.

Mistletoe has its roots in Celtic and Viking celebrations of the season. A parasitic evergreen plant, mistletoe grows high off the ground, tapping into tree trunks and stealing the trees'

> IN THE VIKING-INFLUENCED NORTHERN SCOTTISH ISLANDS, FAMILIES WOULD LOOK FOR ODIN TO COME DURING THE MIDWINTER SOLSTICE . . .

nutrients for its own survival. Nonetheless, in Celtic myth, mistletoe was regarded as a great healer.

In Celtic, mistletoe means "all heal," a name given to the plant believed to possess miraculous healing powers. For ancient Celtic peoples, mistletoe was closely associated with its frequent host, the sacred oak tree. Mistletoe even was thought to hold the soul of the oak.

Druids also saw mistletoe as a plant filled with miraculous possibilities. Mistletoe, it was thought, could heal the sick, neutralize poisons, and make people and animals fertile. It could

also offer protection from witches and their spells, ban evil spirits, and generally ensure good will and good fortune.

Druids made quite a ritual out of cutting and gathering mistletoe. Five days after the new moon following the winter solstice, they would cut the mistletoe from an oak, using a golden sickle. Taking care that nothing was sullied by coming in contact with the ground, Druid priests then divided up the cherished plant among believers eager to gain mistletoe's mysterious protection.

The custom of stealing a kiss under the mistletoe descends, in part, from a Druid tradition. Druids believed that enemies, should they meet under mistletoe, must lay down their arms, greet each other politely, and maintain a truce for one entire day.

The Vikings' admiration for mistletoe and its connection to the holiday season was rooted in Norse mythology. The most beloved of the Norse gods was Balder, the god of beauty, goodness, and light. He was the son of Odin and Frigg. Odin was the chief Norse god. Frigg was the goddess of love. In one Norse legend, Balder is killed by his enemy Loki, the god of evil, with an arrow tipped with poison from the mistletoe plant.

When Balder died, his mother cried and cried, then somehow managed to bring him back to life. Frigg's tears were said to be captured as the white berries of the mistletoe. When her son recovered, she was so happy that she changed the nature of the mistletoe

Odin, ruler of the Norse gods, was an eagerly anticipated visitor in the northern Scottish islands during the midwinter solstice.

from poisonous to healing. Furthermore, she declared that anyone passing beneath mistletoe and sharing a kiss shall be safe from harm. This is another precedent for mistletoe's modern meaning.

ANCIENT VISITORS

Santa wasn't the first visitor to bring presents to children in what is now Scotland. In the Viking-influenced northern Scottish islands, families would look for Odin to come during the midwinter solstice, disguising himself beneath a hooded cloak. Odin would sit by the fire, listen to what people had to tell him, then leave a gift, often money or food, to help those in need.

In the distant past, children in what is now Scotland looked for kindness from their version of Odin, called Woden, the Anglo-Saxon and Celtic god of magic and healing. During the midwinter solstice celebration, Woden would ride to earth on his eight-legged horse, listen to stories from the mortals and hand out good will, good fortune, peace, and presents.

FIRED UP FOR THE HOLIDAYS

Fire is Scotland's most enduring holiday symbol. In ancient Celtic times, the Scottish year was divided into quarters, the arrival of each of the four seasons marked by a fire festival. During days and nights of celebration, bonfires blazed on hillsides, shores, and in the hearts of villages all throughout Scotland.

Fire was most symbolic during the midwinter solstice and new year celebrations. The brightness and heat of the roaring fire served to light the darkness, drive off the forces of evil, and burn up the bad of the past. Then as now, fire was a symbol of celebration in the home. A cozy fire in the hearth at the new year meant warmth, welcome, and prosperity in the year to come. Remnants of Yule logs which burned throughout the season were kept to be used in the holiday fire of the next year.

Up until World War II, many Scottish towns celebrated Hogmanay with a bonfire. Burning a boat was a common New Year's Eve ritual for burning up the old and welcoming the new in seaside villages. Today, a handful of these fire festival traditions continue, drawing huge crowds every year. While many ancient customs have faded over the centuries, fire festivals still fuel the Scottish holiday spirit. As the new year is welcomed in, ancient Scottish fires burn bright.

THE BIGGAR BONFIRE

In the Scottish border town of Biggar, a wild bonfire has burned every New Year's Eve for centuries. The bonfire is allowed by Biggar town authorities and staged by anyone. Wood, coal, and other materials are thrown on the fire to make the bonfire big and keep it burning.

In the past, officials alarmed by the bonfire's size have tried to control the unbridled blaze. However, every request that the fire be contained has been met with cart after cart of wood reinforcements. Once when the Biggar fire brigade extinguished the fire at the "reasonable hour" of 12:30 a.m., the celebrants simply waited until the firemen were gone, relighted the fire, and kept it burning all night as is the tradition.

For hundreds of years without fail, the citizens of Biggar have continued to see the old year out and the new year in with a bonfire. Once during World War II, a group of Biggar residents celebrated New Year's Eve around a single candle in a tin can, keeping the tradition alive without drawing the attention of enemy bombers. On other holidays during the war years, a woman in the town went out and struck a single match at the bonfire site each Hogmanay to ensure the tradition survived.

In recent years, the Biggar bonfire tradition has grown bigger. There is music and dancing around the fire. Then just after 9 p.m. a torchlight procession led by a pipe band makes its way up High Street to the bonfire site in front of Biggar's Corn Exchange.

At 9:30 p.m. everyone sings the Biggar Bonfire Song while the oldest resident of Biggar lights

the fire. Then comes pipe band music and traditional Scottish dances. In the last few minutes before the new year arrives, the assembled crowd quiets to hear the bells at midnight and listens to the final countdown of a lone piper.

The stroke of midnight is greeted with cheers, toasts, kisses all around, more dancing, and stoking the fire to keep it burning strong until the last celebrants head for home.

THE FLAMBEAUX

In Comrie, people celebrate Hogmanay and see in the new year with their own fire festival, the Lighting of the Flambeaux.

The Flambeaux are great, tall torches which have been painstakingly prepared over several weeks leading up to Hogmanay. Small birch trees are chopped down to make long poles, some over 10 feet tall. Each pole is swathed at the top with a torch made of canvas wrapped to the pole with wire and soaked in a large barrel of paraffin.

On New Year's Eve, the torches are placed along the dyke by the Auld Kirkyaird, waiting for the stroke of midnight. When the new year arrives, the torches are lighted with great ceremony. Then, young men take turns shouldering the heavy torches, and with a crowd of people who have gathered in the village square, follow the Comrie Pipe Band in a procession through the village streets. At the end of their march, the torchbearers return to the square. All the torches are heaved into the River Earn.

Stonehaven welcomes in the new year with men parading through the streets after midnight, swinging fireballs.

There is dancing, and prizes are awarded to guisers for the best and most bizarre costumes. "Flambeaux" is French for "beautiful flames," and the name may have been given to the ceremony by Flemish people who lived in the area 200 years ago and taught their style of weaving to the local folk. The custom may go back to an ancient Druid ritual used to chase off witches, or may be related to the Vikings.

STONEHAVEN'S GREAT BALLS OF FIRE

In the Scottish fishing village of Stonehaven, dozens of men welcome in the new year by parading through the streets after midnight, swinging balls of fire over their heads. Made from flammable material packed tightly to burn steadily and bound in a wire cage, each fireball weighs between 16-20 pounds and is held on a 5-foot line.

The ceremony begins when the fireballs are lighted at midnight on Hogmanay. Swinging the blazing balls of fire in circles over their heads, the men walk down High Street all through the town, then down to the harbor. At the end of their march, the men fling the fireballs into the sea.

The townsfolk can trace the tradition back to a fishermen's festival during the 19th century, but its real roots go much deeper into history. As the ceremony is held near the winter solstice, the swinging fireballs may have originally represented the sun. Or the ceremony may be related to a pagan ritual used to drive away witches and evil spirits before the new year begins.

THE BURNING OF THE CLAVIE

At Burghead in Moray, "the Burning of the Clavie" helps usher in the new year on January 11, New Year's Eve according to the old calendar.

The "clavie" is a burning barrel of tar that is carried around town on a post held up by an elected "king." This ancient Scottish fire ceremony ensures good luck and successful fishing in the new year.

Although prohibited by law in 1704, the Burning of the Clavie continues even to this day in Burghead, and has been performed in the same way for hundreds of years. One man is elected Clavie King for the year and a group of about 10 men, traditionally fishermen, are his assistants. The men take a half barrel and fill it with wood shavings and tar. In the past, they used a herring barrel. Today, it's an iron-hooped whiskey barrel coated inside with creosote. The barrel is nailed to the top of a carrying post. This nail is kept and used every year.

The clavie is ceremoniously lighted, using peat from the hearth of an old Burghead provost. The Clavie King and his men take turns carrying the burning clavie as they travel through the streets of Burghead. They stop at various houses to offer a burning faggot from the clavie as a symbol of good luck in the year ahead.

A crowd follows the group of men to Doorie Hill, where they place the clavie on an ancient stone altar. More fuel is piled on to create a huge bonfire. People try to grab flaming embers from the clavie fire to use to start lucky New Year's Day fires at home, or to send to faraway friends and relatives to share in the luck.

CHRISTMAS IN SCOTLAND: THEN AND NOW

Up until the 16th century, Christmas was a lavish, joyous, fun-filled feast day in Scotland, as it was throughout Great Britain. Christmas Day arrived and all work stopped for an extended period of celebration.

Days and nights were filled with preparation and with special rites and traditions, both serious and fun. Friends and family joined in feasting, caroling, and gift-giving. Scotland's lively holiday celebration was a rich swirl of ancient Druid, Celtic, and Nordic rites and Christian traditions of the season.

BIG CHRISTMAS, LITTLE CHRISTMAS, AND DAFT DAYS

In the Celtic language, Christmas was called *Nollaig Mhor*, or "Big Christmas," and the New Year's Day celebration coming one week later was called *Nollaig Beag*, or "Little Christmas." The two celebrations were similar in foods, customs, and traditions, but Big Christmas was the main event.

Christmas became the focus of Scotland's Yule celebration out of respect for Queen Margaret, English wife of Scottish King Malcolm Canmore. In 1066, William of Normandy con-

Christmas in Borthwick Castle

quered England and English Princess Margaret tried to flee, but was shipwrecked on the Scottish coast. Malcolm offered her refuge and married her. The Queen gently brought her new country a touch of Christianity. On Christmas Eve and Christmas Day, solemn masses were said, followed by feasting and festivity. Christmas would remain the focus of the winter season throughout the Middle Ages.

In the distant past, the 12 days from Christmas to Twelfth Night (a period also known as the Yule festival) earned their name as the "Daft Days" in Scotland. There was a carnival atmosphere to the celebration, with plenty of drinking, feasting, merriment, and silliness. "Guisers" (men wearing disguises) and skits mocking the government, the

Scottish minister John Knox reproved Mary Queen of Scots in 1583. He led the Scots in establishing a reformed Protestant national church.

church, and other established orders were allowed as the population let off steam in a big way. This was the one time all year when common folk could break free from the rules of society and live it up—and live it up they did!

THE REFORMATION

In the late 16th century, the fun ended. Before the 1560's, the Roman Catholic Church was the official church of Scotland. Many Scottish leaders resented the Catholic Church's power and France's strong influence on the church. It was during this time that Scottish minister John Knox led the Scots in establishing a reformed Protestant national church. His action occurred about the time that the Reformation spread across northern Europe.

In 1567, Mary, a Catholic, was forced to give up the Scottish throne in favor of her infant son, James VI. Mary fled to England but was captured there and imprisoned. Elizabeth I of England had Mary executed in 1587. James was raised as a Protestant. A reformed Protestant church with a presbyterian form of government by councils of ministers and elders instead of by bishops became firmly established as Scotland's national church during his reign.

THE BATTLE AGAINST CHRISTMAS

The Reformation landed hard on Christmas. Suddenly, everything Roman Catholic had to go. New Protestant rulers regarded all the merry Christmas celebration as "papish" (Roman Catholic), and therefore something that must be stopped.

The battle waged against Christmas celebration was fierce. Christmas was deemed a working day. Anyone taking the day off or giving a holiday to their employees would be fined. Bakers in Scotland who were caught baking Yule breads were fined. Offenders were offered a lighter punishment for turning in the names of their Christmas-celebrating customers. Somber Kirk (Church) of Scotland officials sternly warned parishioners against football games, snowball throwing, singing carols, guising, piping, fiddling, and dancing during the holiday season. Bell ringers walked through towns ordering shops to be opened and men to go to work on Christmas. Schools were ordered not to give their students a Christmas holiday. In 1638, the General Assembly in Edinburgh called for the abolition of the Yule holiday.

AT WAR WITH THE KING

That same year, a group of Scots signed the National Covenant, a pledge to uphold the Church of Scotland and resist changes even when they came from King Charles I. Like his father, James VI of Scotland, who took the title of King James I of England, Charles ruled Scotland and England as separate kingdoms. Thus, the two countries became joined under one king. Charles also continued his father's policies of reorganizing the Scottish church and trying to reintroduce bishops.

In 1642, civil war broke out between Charles and supporters of the English Parliament, many of whom were Puritans. Oliver Cromwell became the leader of the parliamentary forces. The Scottish Covenanters supported the English Parliament in the war. In 1646, Charles surrendered to Scottish forces in England, who turned him over to the English parliamentary forces. The English beheaded him in 1649. Also that

CHRISTMAS TRADITIONS REMAINED STRONG IN DEFIANCE OF THE BAN . . .

year, the General Assembly decided that since the people could not hold Christmas without retaining Yule practice, both should be abolished.

After Charles I's death, the Scots persuaded his son, who later became Charles II, to agree to the National Covenant. They then defied Cromwell and declared Charles II king. But Cromwell defeated Charles's forces in the Battle of Dunbar in 1650. The following year, Cromwell, while occupying Edinburgh, banned Christmas, but the people continued to openly celebrate. In 1654, Cromwell forced the Scots to unite with England.

Charles II finally became king in 1660. He dissolved the union between Scotland and England and, like his father and grandfather, ruled the countries separately.

CHRISTMAS RETURNS TO GREAT BRITAIN

With the restoration of the monarchy in England in 1660, the celebration of Christmas officially returned to Great Britain. Unfortunately, during the silence of the Reformation ban, many of the old rites and traditions of the season had been lost or forgotten.

When the Victorian age arrived, the spirit of Christmas glowed bright once more. In 1840, Queen Victoria's husband Albert introduced the German custom of the Christmas tree to the British royal family celebration. Illustrations of the royal family around their gaily decorated tabletop tree inspired English families rich and poor alike. Quickly, the lavish Victorian celebration of Christmas was in full swing throughout England.

Not so in Scotland. First, the Reformation had banned Christmas celebration as being papish. Now, the dour puritanical Protestants of the Kirk of Scotland found another way to keep Christmas celebration out of Scotland by denouncing the midwinter holiday's pagan roots. It wasn't hard to see the rites of ancient Druid and Celtic solstice festivals and the Nordic Yule mingling in the Christian celebration of the birth of Jesus.

A strict and religious observation of Christmas was prescribed by the Presbyterian Kirk of Scotland. Three days of solemn observance, with work, fasting, and church services squeezed in around business hours, were prescribed. While the rest of Great Britain partied, Christmas remained a somber time in Scotland.

CHRISTMAS UNDERGROUND

Christmas celebration lived on in Scotland—in secret. In the Catholic Highlands Christmas traditions defied the ban. Families put up Christmas trees and sang carols in the privacy of their homes. Scottish children hoped for a visit from St. Nick just as English children did.

Throughout Scotland, Christmas celebration simply "moved" to New Year's Day. "Little Christmas" became very big. The more lively traditions of Christmas shifted to New Year's Day. The Scottish had to behave on Christmas, but they had one grand party on Hogmanay, the Scottish celebration of New Year's Eve and New Year's Day.

The ban on openly celebrating Christmas in Scotland lasted over 400

Christmas decorations adorn St. Magnus Cathedral, Kirkwall, Orkney.

Scottish children hang stockings on Christmas Eve for Santa to fill when he comes down the "lum."

government reorganization made Christmas a public holiday in Scotland.

But the holiday's return has met with resistance from some. With the age-old customs of a Scottish Christmas now buried in the distant past, many Scottish people saw Christmas celebration as merely an English import, or worse, an English tradition intended to rival Hogmanay. Employees of Scottish banks have held strikes protesting being given extra time off at Christmas, the English holiday, rather than at Hogmanay, the Scottish one.

To many of the Scots, Christmas celebration feels foreign and new. When asked about Scottish Christmas traditions, a Scot is likely to say, "Our tradition is not to celebrate Christmas." After a moment's thought, however, he or she may tell you about some traditions that are making their way back into the Scottish celebration of the season.

years. When Christmas finally did come back into public view, it remained religious in focus. There were church services on Christmas Eve and Christmas Day. December 26, the Feast of St. Stephen, now called Boxing Day, was a day for giving to the poor and helping others.

CHRISTMAS RETURNS TO SCOTLAND

It was not until the 1960's that Christmas once again was celebrated openly. Scottish shops were decorated for the season and closed on Christmas Day. Parties were held in church halls, trees and colored holiday lights appeared in public. In the 1970's, local

DECKING THE HALLS

Long before Christmas trees, there were candles and lots of greenery at Christmas in Scotland. An ancient Celtic name for Christmas Eve and for New Year's Eve in Scotland is *Oidche Choinnle*, or "Night of Candles." On Christmas Eve, Scottish families placed candles in windows to light the way for the Holy Family or for any stranger who might come along and want to share in their holiday celebration. The tradition was repeated on New Year's Eve to guide "first-footers" and other visitors. As a gesture of good will, shopkeepers handed out special "Yule candles" to their customers at Christmastime, wishing each shopper, "Fire to warm you by, and a light to guide you."

Holly, mistletoe, rowan, and juniper have been used in Scotland for midwinter holiday decorations since ancient times. Rowan brought luck, holly offered health, mistletoe brought fertility, and juniper gave you a fresh start in the year ahead. In homes, mistletoe was hung in doorways and branches of evergreens and sprigs of holly tucked over picture frames. Juniper and rowan were gathered in vases and spread along mantles.

Holly, important in Roman and Druid winter solstice festivals, has been part of the Scottish midwinter celebration for more than 2,000 years. When Christianity arrived, holly was incorporated into the Christmas celebration. The red berries symbolized the blood of Christ and the evergreen leaves were a sign of everlasting life. Holly also offered shelter to tiny fairies.

Mistletoe was once a pagan symbol banned from church altars and holiday decoration. It was also believed to offer protection from harm or used to designate a truce with enemies. The Victorians brought the magical power of mistletoe back to midwinter celebration. A kiss beneath the mistletoe at Christmas could bring you love or marriage.

A TIME FOR THE WEE BAIRNS

Today, Scottish children hang stockings on Christmas Eve for Santa to fill when he comes down the "lum" and leaves presents under the tree for them to find Christmas morning. Now, the gifts are likely to come from Santa Claus, but Scotland is new to Santa's route. Previously, gifts were given by parents, other family members, and long ago, by other magical December visitors like the Norse God Odin and his Anglo-Saxon counterpart, Woden.

Scottish children eagerly unwrap presents on Christmas morning.

Another old Scottish custom was for children to race to the front door on Christmas morning. To be the first to open the door and welcome in the Yule day and all the goodness it contained was considered very good luck.

CHRISTMAS PUDDING

For some Scottish families, the first taste of the holiday to come is baking the Christmas pudding on the fifth Sunday before Christmas. Traditionally, the entire family helps in the baking, each person taking a turn stirring. The batter is stirred from east to west, symbolizing the journey of the Three Wise Men who came from the East. While you stir, make a secret wish and it will be granted in the year ahead.

The Christmas pudding is an amazing concoction containing raisins, fruits, spices, lard, flour, eggs, carrots, orange juice, and beer or whiskey. Most important, wishwise, is the silver coin mixed in to bring luck to the one who finds it in his or her piece on Christmas Day.

The whole mix is placed in a tin, steamed for seven hours, then stored in a cool place to mature during the weeks before Christmas. When the holiday arrives, the pudding is decorated with a sprig of holly, doused with cognac or whiskey, set on fire, and served.

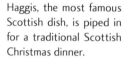

Haggis, the most famous Scottish dish, is piped in for a traditional Scottish Christmas dinner.

A SCOTTISH CHRISTMAS DINNER

The Christmas feast is one tradition that never went away. It might be repeated almost dish for dish on New Year's Day, even turned into a truly lavish Hogmanay spread, but the first feast of the holiday season is, and always was, on Christmas.

The most common main course has changed over time. In the past, a roast goose was traditional for many families. In other homes, Christmas Day meant venison (deer meat) stew. Steak pies also were, and are, a popular choice. Today, the main course is most likely to be roast turkey or chicken.

Other traditional offerings would include root vegetables like "neeps and tatties"—turnips and potatoes. Or, cabbage might be offered, or maybe a mushroom and barley casserole, and, of course, a bowl of Scottish broth.

Many Scottish families cannot let Christmas or New Year's pass without having haggis, that most famous Scottish dish, as part of the holiday meal. Haggis is the stomach of a sheep, stuffed with its chopped lung, liver, and heart mixed with oatmeal and spices, then boiled. Customarily, haggis is served with mashed turnips and whiskey, or "neeps and nips."

While the side dishes may vary, the breads and cakes that grace both the Christmas and New Year's tables are the real essentials, traditions baked according to recipes passed down through the centuries.

Enter a Scottish house on Christmas Day or any day through Hogmanay up

until the very last days of the holiday season and you will be presented with a delicious selection of breads, cakes, buns, shortbread, and cookies spread out on a silver tray or arranged on the table. The choices are rich and delightful.

When you step into the house, however, be sure to have a present of bread or cake and drink for your host tucked under your arm. Though guests will be offered plenty, they must first make an offering of their own. This is because good fortune in the year ahead requires that something come into the house

Today, the Christmas main course in Scotland may be roast turkey or chicken. Traditional offerings include "neeps" and "tatties"—turnips and potatoes, barley casserole, and black bun or Dundee cake for dessert.

(your offering), before anything can be taken away (all you can drink and eat) at Christmas and Hogmanay.

First, there is shortbread, the one simple treat no Scottish family will be without at Christmas or Hogmanay. It's called shortbread, but this really is a sweet cake that is flat and somewhat hard like a bis-

Christmas crackers have traditionally been a popular novelty for Scottish children during the season. These exploding party favors may contain candy, paper hats, and other surprises.

cuit. Shortbread is the modern version of a truly ancient midwinter festival treat.

Following a Scandinavian custom, Scottish families once baked these individual little cakes at the time of the winter solstice. Originally, they were called sun cakes, and were created as part of the celebration of the sun's return and the beginning of a new year. Each cake was round with a hole in the center. "Rays" of the sun were marked out from the middle. Today, these little symmetrical lines that appear on shortbread often are mistaken for convenient slice marks.

Now as in the past, one sumptuous must-have dessert cake for the holidays is black bun. Also called Twelfth Night Cake, this is a dark fruit cake densely filled with dried fruit pieces, almonds and spices, all packed together and soaked with whiskey, then surrounded with a rich pastry and baked in a cake tin. This heady offering is a popular bring-along for first-footers, or to be kept on hand as dessert and for nibbling throughout the holiday season.

Then, there is Dundee cake, the traditional Scottish Christmas cake. This is a light, rising cake with candied fruit pieces and almonds stirred into the batter. Cherry cake is also traditional.

In the past, people of little means were unable to afford meat or rich cakes for their Christmas dinner. Still, they devised ways to make the Christmas meal festive. Oatcakes, spiced up with caraway or cinnamon, were part of the Christmas fare and would be eaten with a special Yule *kebbuck* (cheese). Everyday breads were fancied up with spices and dried fruits for Christmas dinner, too.

A very old, simple, but satisfying food at Christmas in the Scottish countryside was *sowens*. Sowens is a sort of porridge made from the fermented inner husks of oats. A filling staple, sowens was enhanced for Christmas with the addition of honey, black treacle (molasses), and sometimes a dash of whiskey. *Atholl brose*, a sweet Hogmanay drink made from oatmeal mixed with whiskey, cream, honey, and eggs, is a fancy version of this simple food.

In some families, a little round oatcake was baked for each child during the holiday season. Special care was taken with the oatcakes because, while the little cakes brought their owners good luck in the year to come, a cracked or chipped cake was a sign of trouble ahead.

CHRISTMAS WORSHIP

Religious services at Christmas were and are central to the Scottish observance of this special day. People attend church on both Christmas Eve and Christmas Day, and, especially in Roman Catholic families, look forward to the midnight Mass on Christmas Eve.

Christmas is an occasion for many lovely Scottish blessings and prayers, including this Gaelic prayer:

Beannaicht an taigh 's
na bheil ann,
Eadar chuall, is chlac,
is chrann,
Iomair do Dhia, eadar bhrat is
aodach,
Slàinte dhaoine gun robh ann.

which translates:

Bless the house and that which
is in it,
Between rafter and stone
and beam.
Give all to God from rug to linen,
A health to those herein.

Many Scottish families look festive at Christmas dinner in brightly colored party hats found in novelty Christmas crackers.

THE ANIMALS AT CHRISTMAS

In Scotland, people have always lived in close harmony with the creatures that inhabit the rugged and fiercely beautiful landscape of their homeland. From the wild animals of the woodlands and hills, to the fish in the sea, to the livestock in their byre (cow barn), and the pets sleeping by their fireside, all are regarded as essential and deserving of respect and kindness, especially during the Christmas season. Some are even thought to possess magical abilities or do a little fortunetelling at this special time of year.

On Christmas Eve, all the work of a farm must be finished up before Christmas arrives. Extra wood is chopped, all labor is completed because there can be no work on Christmas Day. Following the old custom, there could be no work from Christmas Day through the very end of the holiday season on Twelfth Night.

Most importantly, the livestock must be tended on Christmas Eve. Stalls are freshly cleaned and swept, new hay and extra feed are put out to ensure the animals are well tended now. The same is true on New Year's Eve. All work must be finished before the start of the new year, and work always ends with a trip to the byre or stable to see to the horses and cows, maybe even to say a prayer or special blessing over them this night.

After all, Christmas Eve and New Year's Eve are special nights for the animals as well. At the stroke of midnight on New Year's Eve, cocks would crow and all the cows would groan, according to Scottish beliefs. All the animals were said to kneel for the birth of Jesus on Christmas Eve, and again on New Year's Eve at the moment one year ended and another began.

In Scotland, the bees are known for being busy on Christmas Day. According to a longstanding Scottish belief, bees all leave their hives, swarm around for a spell, then go back in during the early hours of Christmas Day. Many people report they have seen this occur, but no one can say why. Some speculate that the bees hear the noises of people giving special attention to the livestock or coming home from late church services on Christmas Eve and come out to see what the disturbance is. Others guess the bees are themselves joining in the celebration. It is said that if you go up close, you can hear the bees humming in their hives on Christmas Day.

Christmas Day and New Year's Day on a Scottish farm begin with an extra-special meal, maybe an ear of corn, for the horses and cows. Robert Burns' poem "The Auld Farmer's New Year Morning Salutation" captures the special affection of a farmer for his old horse on this occasion:

> A Guid New Year
>   I wish thee, Maggie!
> Hae, there's a ripp (ear of corn)
>   to thy auld baggie
> Tho thou's howe-backit
>   (hump-backed) now, an
>   knaggie (bony)
> I've seen the day
> Thou could hae gaen like
>   onie (any) staggie,
> Out owre the lay (lea, grassy field).

Wild birds are well treated on Christmas Day too. Everywhere in Scotland, it is the custom to put out food for the birds at Christmas. In the past, crofters (cultivators of small farms) would put out a special offering of seeds or bread for birds this day.

LOOK TO THE ANIMALS FOR LUCK

You can learn a lot from the animals you see on New Year's Day in Scotland. The first creature you see when you look out the window or step out the door on New Year's Day predicts how your year will go. Should you see a dead animal first, that signals bad things to come—not to mention a bad thing right now. An animal lying down in the field also is not a good sign. You want to see animals facing you, not offering you a tail. To see a cow or horse standing and walking or running toward you is best of all and symbolizes good things to come.

Birds flying can be a bad thing because they indicate that a person is planning to move away or leave the country soon. Then again, a bird sitting very still is said to signal that a bad thing is about to happen.

In the past, people would go to great lengths to safeguard their livestock from ill will on the first day of a new quarter of the year, and most especially on the first day of the quarter that begins a brand-new year. Fire, water, ammonia, urine, salt, prayers, and chants were burned, sprinkled, tossed, whispered, and sung, all with the purpose of protecting a family's animals.

Then, there are all the regular

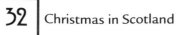

dangers that might befall livestock during the year ahead. To head off trouble now, a farmer would take his own New Year's oatcake out into the field. He would sit on the ground and, as he ate the cake, toss pieces over his shoulder, saying, "Here to thee, wolf, spare my sheep; there to thee, fox, spare my lambs; here to thee eagle, spare my goats; there to thee, raven, spare my kids; here to thee, marten, spare my fowls; there to thee, harrier, spare my chickens."

Farmers were sure to keep a close watch on their flocks, herds, and even dogs and cats on the very first day of the year. Animals you let get away on New Year's Day will go and never come back, it was said.

You especially would want to keep your cat in at night all through the magical Christmas holiday sea-son. Otherwise, fairies who are out doing mischief might catch the cat and ride around on it. On New Year's morning, though, some people throw a cat—or a duck or any other handy small animal, but never a dog—out the door first thing in the morning. Walking away, this "scape" animal would take with it all the bad luck of the year before.

THE CANDLEMASS BULL

At the very end of the Christmas season comes the Candlemas Bull. Candlemas, February 2, is celebrated as the day the Virgin Mary first presented the baby Jesus at the temple and is the very last official day related to Christmas celebration. The bull that comes this day isn't re-ally a bull, but a bull that has taken shape as a cloud. People watched this "bull" travel across the sky to learn whether they would have a good or poor year for crops. A bull traveling east was good, but if it faced west, things would go badly. This tradition comes down from an ancient Scots religion but has lasted because it was so strong a belief and because it was tied to a modern religious observance.

The first fish caught in the new year was a lucky omen along the Scottish coast. In the fishing villages, men would compete to be the first to throw out a line and the first to "draw blood" in the new year. If rough weather prevented heading out in fishing boats, the men would go hunting to shoot an animal, again trying to be first to kill something.

Highland cows graze on the shore of Loch Etive, near Connel.

HOGMANAYS OF AULD

A guid new year to ane an' a'
An' monie may ye see,
An' during a' the years to come
O happy may ye be
An' may ye ne'er hae cause to mourn,
To sigh or shed a tear.
To ane an' a baith great an' sma'
A hearty guid new year.

It's the first of many wish-filled verses of "A Guid New Year," a Scottish Hogmanay song that will be sung with gusto on the streets and in homes everywhere this night.

In past times, Celtic people figured the new year began with the winter before a spring. In the same way, each day really began with its eve. Hogmanay, the big, rousing Scottish celebration of the new year, begins at midnight and continues through the wee hours of a cold, dark Scottish winter night.

A CLEAN SWEEP

But first, there is real work to do. Everything and everyone must be made ready for a new year ahead. In a country where the beginning of each new quarter of the year was re-

Hogmanay celebration
in Edinburgh, 1876

garded as a fresh start and a chance to do things right, the first moment of a whole new year was the most serious sort of new beginning.

Before the new year arrives, you must make a clean sweep, literally. Your house must be scrubbed from top to

In the Highlands and islands, New Year's Eve is sometimes called *Oidhche Chaluinne*, which means "Night of the Candles."

bottom. Everything about the house must be made new and right. Walls are washed or painted; pots and pans are polished to a shine; floors are swept; the front steps are scrubbed; curtains are washed; and windows are cleaned.

Nothing can be left untended or in an unfinished state. All washing, sewing, and weaving must be finished. Wood is chopped and stacked. Baking for the entire holiday season must be completed.

The barn and animals need to be ready for the new year, too. Stalls are cleaned and swept. Fences are mended. Carts, boats, and all work tools are repaired and put in their proper places.

Business and personal matters must all be put right. Bills and debts must all

be paid or collected. Borrowed items must be returned. Arguments must be settled and slights forgiven. It is important to approach the new year and the new beginning it represents with a clean slate, a clear conscience, and a peaceful heart.

Now is also the time to deal with any nastiness lurking about. To permit good fortune to enter in the year ahead, it is essential to drive out any lingering bad influences of the year passing. In the past, smoke from juniper branches sometimes was used as an extreme measure to "fumigate" the house and barn of all evil forces. Walking from room to room with burning juniper on the first day of the new year, the head of the house would fill every corner with smoke, causing much coughing and wheezing, but getting the job done.

Finally, everything is ready. In the very last moments of the old year, people throw open their windows and doors, bang on pots and pans, blow horns and whistles, shout, and shoot off guns as a final measure to drive away all the misfortune and evil the year contained.

HOGMANAY ARRIVES

New Year's Eve in Scotland goes by several names. In Gaelic, and especially in the Highlands and islands, it's sometimes called *Oidhche Chaluinne*, which means "Night of the Candles." This name comes from the candles placed in windows to welcome strangers and visitors and light their way this night. In rural Fife and the surrounding area,

New Year's Eve sometimes is called "Singin' E'en" because this is the old traditional night for Yuletide caroling.

Then, there is Hogmanay, the one name every Scottish person knows for the one celebration no Scottish person would ever want to miss. The word Hogmanay stands for the celebration on New Year's Eve. It is also the name for presents and cakes given on this night, and for the entertainment provided on New Year's Eve.

As the clock strikes midnight on New Year's Eve, a Scottish family shares toasts, kisses, hugs, and handshakes. Then, it is traditional to hold hands or dance around the table, singing:

Weel may we a' be,
Ill may we never see,
Here's to the king
And the guid companie!

Young men of the family next load up a supply of drinks, buns, and breads and head out to "first foot" the houses of their neighbors, friends, and relatives, sometimes walking for miles to offer New Year's wishes all around (see "First-Footers," pg.42-43). At each home, they hope to be invited in to share delicious Hogmanay food and drink and warm themselves by the fire.

Many young men, and in more recent times, women, too, leave their homes well before midnight to join the gathering at the village square, the *mercat cross* (market cross), a central church, or the town hall. In every Scottish city or town, there is one special place where everyone meets to see the New Year in together. In Edinburgh, it is the Tron Kirk (town hall) in the middle of the Royal Mile; in Stirling, it is the Steeple at the

At the close of the Hogmanay party in Scotland, everyone comes together in a circle to sing "Auld Lang Syne." During the last verse, everyone crosses their arms and links hands all around.

top of King Street; in Dundee, the city square; in Aberdeen, Union Street in front of the Town House; and in Glasgow, it is Glasgow Cross.

Here, the crowd waits together for the town clock to strike midnight or for the church bells to ring in the new year. Then, wild cheers erupt, and with plenty of singing, kissing, and toasting from the bottles they're carrying to "first-foot" later, the new year is welcomed.

These days, groups of friends and relations set out together to visit each one's home to share a toast and bring good luck in the year ahead. At the end of the tour, they all end up at one designated home for a big Hogmanay dinner and party. After the stroke of midnight, after the toasts and songs, many friends and families exchange gifts which they call Hogmanays.

AULD LANG SYNE

After kisses and toasts all around at midnight and again when the Hogmanay party—or any important Scottish celebration—comes to a close, it's traditional to sing "Auld Lang Syne." Around the world, this sweet old Scottish song has come to symbolize feelings of remembered friendships, family, and home on New Year's Eve.

The words to the song are written in old Scots, the primary language that was spoken in Scotland until 1707 when Scotland's Parliament was dissolved and Scotland's government was joined with England's. *Auld Lang Syne* translates as "Old Long Ago" and that's about all the Old Scots you really have to know to get the right feeling

and join in the singing on this special night.

In 1788, the beloved Scottish writer Robert Burns penned the words we still sing today. He based his rendition on an ancient melody and various verses that were in print for at least 80 years before he added his special touch.

In Scotland, everyone comes together in a circle for "Auld Lang Syne." The last verse begins, "And there's a hand my trusty fiere. And gie's a hand o' thine." Now, everyone crosses their arms and links hands all around, singing full out, with spirit, and moving in and back from the circle's center or swaying side to side.

FOOD AND DRINK

Traditional Hogmanay fare is rich, sweet, and warming to the spirit. All the foods served at Christmas also are customary at Hogmanay, with the addition of one special dessert. The English have their plum pudding. In Scotland, the Hogmanay meal-ending delight is called *clootie dumpling*. A sweet cake with raisins and spices, the dumpling is cooked in a cloth and boiled in a pot of water for about four hours, then allowed to dry.

Guests at any house on Hogmanay and *Ne'er's Day* (New Year's Day) also can expect to be offered an array of rich and tasty cakes, including shortbread, black bun, cherry cake, and plum cake, sultana cake, seed cake, and oatcakes.

In Scotland, just as there are holiday toasts, there are very special holiday drinks. First, there is the *het pint*, the

AULD LANG SYNE

Should auld acquaintance be forgot,
And never brought to mind?
Should auld acquaintance be forgot,
And auld lang syne?

[CHORUS]
For auld lang syne, my dear,
For auld lang syne,
We'll tak' a cup o' kindness yet
For auld lang syne!

And surely ye'll be your pint-stowp (tankard),
And surely I'll be mine,
And we'll tak' a cup o' kindness yet
For auld lang syne!

[CHORUS]
We twa (two) *hae run about the braes* (hills),
And pou'd (pulled) *the gowans* (daisies) *fine,*
But we've wander'd monie (many) *a weary fit* (foot)
Sin' auld lang syne.

[CHORUS]
We twa hae paidl'd (paddled) *in the burn* (stream)
Frae morning sun (noon)
  till dine (dinner/evening time),
But seas between us braid (broad) *hae roar'd*
Sin' auld lang syne.

[CHORUS]
And there's a hand, my trusty
  fiere (friend),
And gie's a hand o' thine,
And we'll tak' a right guid-willie
  waught (good swig of drink)
For auld lang syne!

[CHORUS]
For auld lang syne, my dear,
For auld lang syne,
We'll tak' a cup o' kindness yet
For auld lang syne!

Scottish national poet Robert Burns penned the words to "Auld Lang Syne" in 1788 that we still sing today.

traditional first-footer's drink, carried house to house in a copper kettle. This steaming, spiced mulled ale is the perfect drink to warm the spirits while toasting in the new year.

Another Hogmanay tradition is *Atholl brose*. This very sweet Scottish treat combines Scotland's best ingredients: oatmeal, whiskey, cream, honey, and eggs. Usually prepared as a drink, Atholl brose also can be made thick enough to serve as a dessert with whipped cream on top. Atholl brose must be prepared at least a week in advance of your Hogmanay celebration.

If you can't prepare a home-made drink, don't arrive without something under your arm or greet guests without something to serve. At Hogmanay, even year-round teetotalers will have a dram to toast the new year. A bottle of the whiskey for which Scotland is famous is always appropriate.

For children and anyone preferring nonalcoholic toasts, the traditional Hogmanay drink is ginger wine, made by boiling lemons, oranges, sugar, and water together with ginger and other spices.

HOGMANAY LADS

In the past, New Year's Eve was one of the times when groups of men and boys went out caroling and collecting food and treats.

One of the most colorful groups afoot on New Year's Eve were the "Hogmanay Lads." One boy wearing a calf's

> WHATEVER ITS ORIGINAL MEANING, HOGMANAY IS A TERM WORLD FAMOUS AS THE NAME OF THE GRAND SCOTTISH NEW YEAR'S EVE CELEBRATION

hide and several others carrying sticks and bags would arrive at your door. The boys would start their routine by circling the house, "beating" the calf and their bags with the sticks, and singing a request to be welcomed in.

Once inside, the boy in the calf skin would head straight to the fire. He would singe the end of his cowhide tail, then walk around the room, letting each person sniff the smoking hair for good luck. Sometimes, the group leader also circled the head of the woman of the house with the tail three times for good luck.

In some places, the calfskin wearer recited his Hogmanay poem while walking in a circle in the house as the inhabitants tried to hit him with a broom. In other places, all the boys would walk around the house's fire, bringing luck to the dwelling and everyone in it. The boys' reward for bringing good fortune, and for escaping harm, was food and drink, plus cakes to put in their sacks. If the boys were refused entrance to a home or denied gifts of food, they would recite a curse and build a little blockade in front of a person's cottage.

GUISERS

Plenty of other interesting groups were out making the rounds on New Year's Eve, as well as on Christmas Eve, New Year's Day, and all through the holiday season. They were "guising" or "mumming"—carrying on a very old holiday custom which was popular throughout Northern Europe, and especially in Scotland. Friends would call on friends, but guising also was a way the poor could go house to house, visiting the well-to-do and asking for a share of their bounty.

At Christmastime, "guisers" would don strange costumes and walk from house to house, performing at each door to receive a reward of some kind. Guisers were often men or boys dressed as women or wearing their clothing inside out. Others wore all white or blacked their faces in disguise. In the Shetland Islands, costumed carolers called *skeklers*, or *grulicks*, came to your door wearing large white shirts covered with straw, their faces hidden under white cloths.

Some guisers performed a little skit for their hosts and were dressed for the part. Others played pipes and drums, sang, and entertained merrily. All of them expected be invited in for cheese, bread, black bun, shortbread, and a dram of whiskey at every stop.

The songs and rhymes offered by the Hogmanay guisers were many and varied. Some were short and straight to the point, as in:

My feet's cauld, my
  shoon's thin;
Gie's my cakes, and let
  me rin!

Others could go on verse after verse, offering the friendliest kind of New Year's wish. Sometimes, a charming verse might end with a veiled threat of mischief to those who didn't open doors or offer treats, such as one long rhyme which contains the final verse:

Let each give me bannock
  (Hogmanay cake or
treat),
That the New Year may go
  well with you.
May he who give no bannock
Have his reward from Donald
the dark and bad (the devil).

On leaving a friendly house, the guisers might sing a final rhyme of blessing, such as:

God bless the master of this
  house,
And mistress also,

Likewise the little bairnies
  (children),
That round the table go.
May your purse be full of money,
Your cellars full of beer,
We wish you many a Hogmanay,
And many a good New Year.

HOGMANAY: ORIGINS OF THE WORD

In the distant past, the people of Scotland spoke two languages, Gaelic in the Highlands and on the islands west of the mainland; and Old Scots, which was somewhat similar to Old English, in the Lowlands. Where does the word *Hogmanay* originate? Maybe from Gaelic or Old Scots—or maybe from any of a number of other intriguing sources. No one knows for sure, but it's fun to speculate.

Some possibilities to consider:

- Hogmanay could be a more modern version of *oge maidne*, a Gaelic term meaning "new morning."
- There is an ancient Scots accounting term meaning "hog money." This was also the name of one of the earliest types of coins.
- Or, *haleg monath*, an Anglo-Saxon term meaning "holy month."
- The ancient Greeks spoke of *Hagmena* or *ôhagmena*, meaning "holy moon." The Druids used this name for their ceremony for cutting the sacred mistletoe.
- *Hoggo-nott*, *Hagenat*, or *Hogg-night* are versions of the Scandinavian word for the night before the feast of Yule.
- The Flemish offer *hoog min dag*, three words which together mean "great love day."

The French language offers a number of strong contenders. These all are supported by the former strong ties in songs and customs between Scotland and France.

- First, *homme est né*, French for the phrase "Man is born."
- *Aguillaneuf* is also a French word. This is an old French name for the last day of the year and for the gifts given then.
- *Hoguinané*, which is a Norman French version of Aguillaneuf.
- Another French phrase, *au gui mener*, means "lead to the mistletoe" and seems to sound right and fit the occasion.
- Finally, there is *hoguignetes*, another French term. This one from Normandy describes the presents given on New Year's Day.

Whatever its original meaning, *Hogmanay* is a term world famous as the name of the grand Scottish New Year's Eve celebration and all its trappings.

FIRST-FOOTERS

As the clock ticks off the final few moments of the passing year on December 31, any misfortune or unhappiness that year can be forcibly driven from your home. All you have to do is fling your doors and windows open wide and usher out all bad spirits with wild shouting, banging on pans, blowing whistles and horns, and shooting off guns.

Luck for the new year enters with the household's "first-footer," the first person to cross the threshold in the new year. The Hogmanay first-footer is Scotland's most celebrated and enduring tradition. First-footing is an ancient tradition, predating Christian celebrations of the season. In the past, following the dictates of the seasonal calendar, Scots watched for first-footers and the good or bad luck they would bring not just on New Year's Day, but on the first Monday of every quarter of the year.

What determines a lucky first-footer? A happy year ahead arrives with a tall, dark-haired man, preferably handsome, preferably a stranger. To bring good luck, the first-footer must bring a drink to share and other customary gifts for the family and the home.

Traditional, symbolic first-footer gifts are a drink to warm the spirits; a lump of coal to warm the house; shortbread, black bun, oatcakes, or all three, depending on the region of Scotland, to feed the family; and a

coin or salt to bring prosperity. In some places, a first-footer might bring a sheaf of corn. In Dundee, first-footers traditionally brought along a red herring tied with a ribbon.

In the old days, the traditional drink carried by a first-footer was called *het pint*. This steaming-hot homemade concoction of ale mulled with nutmeg and whiskey was carried from house to house in a copper kettle. Other drinks might be substituted, but the drink selected must be suitable for a toast and for warming spirits. First-footers making the rounds would share a drink from the kettle with every friend they met and offer a dram—a small drink—to the host in every home they entered.

Upon arriving at a home, a first-footer announces, "A guid New Year to ane' and a', and monie may ye see"("A good New Year to one and all, and many may you see"), "A happy New Year tae ye, and God's blessing," or some similar greeting. The first-footer offers a dram to his host and receives one in return, toasts with the family all around, kisses every woman, and is in-

vited to join in the Hogmanay feast and celebration.

Every group of arriving friends will come prepared to "first-foot" you, bringing a drink to share and luck for the year ahead, whether they are first at your door or not.

The first person to cross your threshold in the new year is believed to determine a familiy's luck for the year. It is customary for first-footers to carry with them a drink or other gift for the family and home.

These days, first-footers offer a dram from a bottle of whiskey, the new traditional stand-in for the homemade het pint. Lumps of coal and measures of salt generally have been dropped by the wayside, coins are pocketed, but shortbread, black bun, or oatcakes are welcome—and they are expected, along with boxes of chocolates, fruit, and other little gifts, as people everywhere first-foot their friends.

In Lanark, the tradition of the het pint at New Year's lives on in the annual ceremony of the het pint. On the first morning of the new year, old folks in the town are welcome to visit the local district council office and receive a pound note and a glass of beer.

First-footing begins in the early minutes of the new year. As the clock approaches midnight on New Year's Eve, young men have gathered at the designated spot in any city or village, typically outside the town kirk or town hall or in the city square, to celebrate together when the bells ring in the new year. In Edinburgh, the Tron Kirk was the traditional center of such celebration.

After a few rousing cheers, toasts, singing and handshakes all around, the men would then set off to first-foot all their friends and relations, armed with a good supply of drink, buns, cakes, coal, coins, and the like. Stopping at every house to bring good luck and share a drink to the new year meant a full night of fun, joining in one Hogmanay celebration after another. Today, after celebrating with thousands in the streets of Edinburgh, Glasgow, and elsewhere, people still take their leave to first-foot at all-night Hogmanay parties in the homes of their friends.

Why is a tall, dark-haired man the best choice for a first-footer? This may be because in the past, a tall, blonde stranger at your door was likely to be a raiding Viking, a visitor who brought the very worst sort of luck.

But no matter how tall, dark, and even handsome a first-footer may be, if he arrives empty-handed, he will be unwelcome for he brings bad luck. To arrive at a doorstep without a drink to share is considered a terrible insult, the same as wishing a curse on the family for the coming year.

Traditionally, any stranger appearing at the door on Hogmanay was heartily welcomed in to share a toast, have something to eat, and warm themself in the glow of Scottish hospitality and a roaring fire. These days in Scotland, inviting in a total stranger is more rare, even on New Year's Eve. First-footers are likely to be friends.

According to tradition, a woman first-footer means real trouble in the year ahead. This was not a common problem, because women traditionally hosted the Hogmanay parties and waited for visitors.

In the past, flat-footed first-footers were considered unlucky. So, too were pious, sanctimonious people. In various parts of Scotland, other unlucky first-footers include: a person with eyebrows that meet, a lame leg, a blind eye, turned-out or turned-in toes, red hair, fair skin, or dark skin.

You also did not want to meet at your door: A midwife, gravedigger, hangman, thief, doctor, minister, anyone dressed too poorly or too well, or a stingy or immoral person. A poor, old woman asking for kindling was considered terribly unlucky. And be on your guard if the first-footer is a witch or a bearded woman.

Along with a dark-haired man, some other first-footers are considered especially lucky. A woman, on the condition that she is barefooted, can be good. Children are good, and so are all generous people and good-looking people. Hearty, merry fellows, people free from association with witchcraft, and anyone born feet first are welcome. And, while in some places they are considered unlucky first-footers, people with dark skin, fair skin, or red hair are considered lucky in other places.

Animals also bring luck this day. A dog is a very lucky first-footer. A first-footing cat is bad luck. People traveling about first-footing this night had to be especially watchful regarding animals they might encounter this night. A rabbit running across your path is bad, as is a cat running straight before you—or doing anything at all. You also don't want to see a frog, a toad, a pig, or a mouse first or hear a crow cry. Meeting up with a dog, cow, or horse first thing on your trip, however, would be good.

Today, the tradition of the first-footer is more about fun than fortunetelling. People set out to "first-foot" each other's homes, bringing along a bottle, shortbread and buns, small gifts of all kinds, and their warmest wishes for the new year. After midnight, every family sends out first-footers to their friends and waits for friends and family to bring good luck their way, too. All this first-footing makes Hogmanay a truly shared celebration.

HOGMANAY AND NE'ER'S DAY TODAY

The Scottish people treasure their Hogmanay celebration for the one-of-a-kind New Year's welcome that it is. These days, that welcome is bigger, brighter, and merrier than ever.

In recent years, rather than being allowed to diminish and fade away like many ancient traditions before it, Hogmanay has been given a boost of fresh vigor. Just as the number of first-footers who traditionally gathered at the Tron Kirk in Edinburgh began to dwindle, Hogmanay celebration was kicked into high gear. Now, hundreds of thousands crowd the streets of Edinburgh, Glasgow, Stirling, Inverness, and Scottish cities and villages of every size to count down the last minutes in a joyous, new, all-out version of Hogmanay.

The first brand new, revved-up Hogmanay celebration occurred in 1992, when Edinburgh staged a citywide Hogmanay party as a special treat for the European Union Heads of State Conference being hosted in the city. Thousands of people filled the capital's streets, kissed, hugged, sang, danced all night, and toasted in a powerful Hogmanay rebirth. Each year now, the Edinburgh Hogmanay

Hundreds of thousands of revelers from all over the world travel to Edinburgh for the big Hogmanay celebration on New Year's Eve.

party grows, and so do New Year's bashes in cities and villages across Scotland. People fly in from all over the world to be on the street in Edinburgh or in front of the castle in Stirling when the bells and fireworks signal the start of a new year.

Hogmanay parties stretch on for days, include street theater, dancing, and all kinds of events, and make welcome every person, young and old. For safety's sake, passes have had to be issued in recent years to limit the thousands entering various street parties in Edinburgh and Glasgow.

The passes are free. Half the passes are reserved for Edinburgh residents; the rest are available to anyone who writes requesting them. In the world-famous Scottish spirit of hospitality, there's something for everyone, all are welcome, and the more the merrier at citywide Hogmanay celebrations. While some special shows have limited, paid admission, the top-billed musicians and artists who perform are likely to join the general party afterward, taking to the street to put on additional impromptu performances free of charge.

In recent years, the emphasis has been on making sure the Hogmanay parties—even those that have grown into gigantic events—remain truly Scottish celebrations. There are rock bands and strange street theater, but there is always plenty of traditional fiddle and drum music, and the "whirl and skirl" of Scottish dancing, plus torchlight processions and other fire festival customs. *Ceilidh*, traditional Scottish dances, are held in castles, on stages, and in the street.

Traditional ceilidh dances also are held in barns and community centers all across the country on Hogmanay. Away from the center of the city, up in the Highlands, on the islands, and out in the countryside, Hogmanay celebration still takes the shape it did hundreds of years ago. In remote areas, people still walk miles to first-foot their neighbors and see the new year in right.

EDINBURGH'S GRAND HOGMANAY

At a population of approximately 450,000, compared to Glasgow's 750,000, the capital city of Edinburgh isn't the largest city in Scotland, but it hosts the grandest Hogmanay bash.

Passes for the Edinburgh Hogmanay street party first were issued after the 1996-97 event when over 300,000 people showed up and the crowd was too large to manage safely. Now, only 180,000 passes are given out, keeping the total number of revelers to around 200,000 who make their way into the restricted area of the street party. At that number, the party also requires around 400 performers, 1,200 police and festival officials, and creates 93 tons of litter.

Given the unpredictable nature of Scottish winter weather, the Edinburgh celebration has sometimes proved to be a party for the hearty. Pouring rains and howling winds showed up for the 2001 New Year's celebration. So did 100,000 Hogmanay celebrants. The rain continued and the party went on. The revelers were drenched, but their Hogmanay spirits refused to be dampened.

The schedule of events changes every year as the Edinburgh organizers challenge themselves to make the next Hogmanay even better than the last. Still, the most important elements are guaranteed. There will be a grand torchlight procession, more than one street party, and, at the stroke of midnight, a colossal fireworks display above Edinburgh Castle perched high on a volcanic rock overlooking the city.

Five days and nights of celebrating open on the evening of December 27 with a traditional torchlight procession and fire festival. It all begins at Edinburgh Castle where torches are sold to benefit Scottish charities. In the procession, the hundreds of torch bearers are led by costumed historical figures like Mary Queen of Scots and her standard bearers, and escorted by a number of pipe and drum bands.

Many of the men at this *ceilidh* wear kilts. A ceilidh is a traditional Scottish dance.

A torchlight procession pulls a Viking longboat at the Beltane Festivities in Edinburgh.

party which gives the younger set a chance to join in the dancing and celebrating before things get wilder and louder on New Year's Eve.

On Ne'er's Eve itself, the revelers come early and stay late to see the new year in with dancing and partying in the chilly night air. As midnight approaches, everyone waits for the countdown. Just after the crowd shouts out the last second of the old year, cathedral bells ring in the new year as a spectacular fireworks display lights up the night sky over Edinburgh Castle, illuminating the ancient hilltop fortress. In 2000, fireworks were launched from Edinburgh Castle and from six other hills around the city. There is plenty of hugging and kissing, handshaking, and a chorus or two of "Auld Lang Syne." Then, it's hours of more music and dancing for some and off to first-foot friends and family at private parties for others.

GLASGOW GIVES IT A GO

Glasgow, Scotland's biggest city, is host to the country's second biggest Hogmanay party—but that could change anytime. Year after year, the competition is on as Glasgow tries to wrestle the best Hogmanay bash title away from Edinburgh. More than 100,000 revelers take to the streets of Glasgow for all-night music and fun on New Year's Eve. With multiple street parties and multiple stages for performers, there's something for every taste.

For a recent Glasgow Hogmanay celebration, music offerings ranged from traditional Scottish fiddle bands to "a

In the past, the marchers would then drag a Viking long boat through the city to Calton Hill. The torches then were tossed on the boat and everyone watched as it burned. In more recent years, the procession of torches, without a boat, has traveled from the Castle down the Royal Mile past Holyrood Palace and to the nearby park where the torches light a bonfire. Here, there is also music, fire sculptures, and fireworks.

Over the next few days, events for families, plays, concerts, and choir performances at the city's cathedrals are planned, all leading up to the December 31 Hogmanay Street Party. On the night of December 30, kids hit the streets first for a family-oriented street

Celtic reggae fusion" band, to the Glasgow Community Gospel Choir, to a popular teen rock band, to salsa. There was a street circus including a Chinese lion dance and giant skeleton puppets, a comedy stage and more.

STIRLING JOINS THE FUN

When more than 20,000 people filled the streets to welcome in the new millennium at Stirling's first official citywide Hogmanay party, the city knew it had a brand new tradition on its hands.

These days, you need a ticket to attend the Stirling Castle "main event" party with "Celtic folk-rocksters" and all kinds of fiddle bands on the program. However, there is plenty more fun to be had out in the streets at two public parties featuring everything from rock bands to Scottish fiddlers, and lots of dancing, all for free. To round things out, a ceilidh is held at the Albert Halls. Stirling Castle provides the dramatic setting for fireworks at midnight.

For the children, an afternoon "Hogmanay Hooley" will have stilt-walking, theater, puppets, dancing, and more. New Year's Day in Stirling will offer a selection of sporting events and still more dancing.

MORE HOGMANAY FUN

Dundee's Hogmanay celebration is focused on family fun. There is no rip-roaring street party. Instead, an afternoon of street theater and music in the City Centre and other shopping areas is coupled with demonstrations by lo-

cal artists. At the Dundee Ice Arena, skaters take to the ice until midnight. Elsewhere, the Hogmanay Cycle Ride is on. Finally, the new year is greeted with a fireworks display at midnight.

Inverness, which calls itself the capital of the Highlands and islands, also presents a family-oriented Hogmanay celebration. The afternoon and early evening of December 31 are filled with street theater, a fun fair and other activities for children, plus traditional Scottish dancing. In the early evening, the Riverlights display is turned on to light River Ness like thousands of stars falling from the clear skies. Then, families and friends are off to parties in homes, clubs, and hotels, returning just before midnight to see an explosion of fireworks over Inverness Castle.

Today, Scotland's various Hogmanay celebrations draw revelers from

Revelers of all ages participate in Edinburgh's Viking longboat pulling torchlight procession on December 27.

Many Scottish areas, like the west coast town of Oban, Argyll, *above*, celebrate New Year's Eve with fireworks.

around the world. Months in advance of the party night, official Hogmanay Web sites keep the world up to date with the latest information about special events and performances, where to write for passes to street parties, and how to find accommodations, plus street maps showing party and event sites, weather advisories, helpful tips, and transportation guides. Coveted passes for the Edinburgh street parties are snapped up early. Those eager to be in the main action at Hogmanay get requests in by the early fall. Others join "first-foot" clubs to assure a chance at a pass closer to the cutoff date.

During Hogmanay itself, streaming Webcam broadcasts and television coverage offer anyone anywhere a chance to see the fireworks at midnight over Inverness Castle or Edinburgh Castle and bring viewers at home right up close to the action in the streets all across Scotland.

NE'ER'S DAY

You would think Ne'er's Day—New Year's Day in Scotland—would be a national nap day, considering the all-night Hogmanay hoopla of the night before. Instead, it is a day packed with activity and filled with holiday traditions. In fact, the city-sponsored Hogmanay festivals of the night before are still in progress along with new events for the day's schedule.

The competition this day begins right away with who can get out of bed first. According to Scottish tradition, first up is a prize worth winning. Then, rugby, football, soccer, golf, and many other kinds of ball games are afoot today. There are family matches, team matches, and games where entire towns are in on the action (see Chapter 5, "Holidays on the Scottish Islands," page 54 and "Highland Holiday Fun and Games," page 53).

Then, there are some wild sports

that only the bracing spirit of the first day of the new year can inspire. In Edinburgh, Holyrood Park is the site for some new traditional Ne'er's Day activities. First comes Huskies at Holyrood, sled-dog racing around the crags of Holyrood Park. Then there is the Ne'er's Day Edinburgh Bicycle Co-op New Year's Triathlon with a 400-meter swim, 11-mile cycle ride, and 3.5-mile run around Arthur's Seat (one of Edinburgh's many hills) in the park.

Not daring enough for you? Join the determined crew for the annual Loony Dook (dunk), a New Year's Day plunge into the icy waters of the Firth of Forth at South Queensferry, just outside Edinburgh.

If you aren't up to sports today, Edinburgh also offers concerts at St. Mary's Cathedral, performances by the Scottish Chamber Orchestra, gallery and art fair exhibits, and even a little street theater at Hunter Square.

Dundee holds its own "Ne'er's Day Dook." Organized by Ye Amphibious Ancients Bathing Association, the Dundee dook takes place at 1:30 p.m., depending on the tide, at Broughty Pier, Broughty Ferry, Dundee.

Stirling's Hogmanay celebration continues on New Year's Day with a First Foot Forward Fun Run and finishes up this evening with The Final Fling, a traditional Scottish dance, all ages welcome, in the Great Hall at Stirling Castle.

NE'ER'S DAY DEVILMENT

Just as Hogmanay is famous for its many treats, New Year's Day is a time for tricks. Devilment is the name the Scottish give to pranks and practical jokes, and there is plenty of it to go around now. Especially, this is the time for children and teens to play tricks on adults.

Erecting blockades was an old favorite trick. Boys would collect the wagons and carts belonging to all the neighbors and use them to make a blockade in the center of town. Or they would gather up all of a farmer's carts, wheelbarrows, and plows to make a blockade in front of his cottage door. In seaside villages, boats would be dragged from the beaches and used to block doorways and streets.

Sometimes parts of boats or necessary farm equipment would be missing in the morning. Families would wake up on New Year's morning to find their windows boarded up or bricked in. A simple but very nasty trick was to use a large piece of peat to block a house's chimney. During the night, street signs

Each New Year's Day, brave souls take a dip in the icy waters of the Firth of Forth at South Queensferry for the annual Loony Dook.

would be switched all over town.

Another popular trick was to take the mortar-stone from the front door of a young woman the young men wished to see get married in the year to

come. Sometimes one special, and large, stone was used and carried to the house of a different young woman's family each New Year's Day.

THIGGING FOR OTHERS

While the boys were running around making mischief, groups of young men would travel about on New Year's Day with only good intentions. On this morning, small groups of men would go *thigging*, begging not for themselves, but for an old man or woman, an invalid, or some other needy person.

Walking for miles sometimes, the *thiggers* would stop at every house, offer a song, and ask, "Are ye gueede for beggars?"

To this, the reply would be, "Fah are ye beggin' for?"

The men would identify the person they wanted to help, be given money and food for their cause, and set off again. Invitations to come in, eat, and enjoy the company were politely refused, with "Na, na, sittin' beggars canna speed."

BEGGING FOR BANNOCKS

Ne'er's Day also was a day for children to go from house to house dancing, singing, and begging for their "hogmanay," a treat for the new year.

A family had to be sure to have lots of extra little oatcakes on hand. Shortbread or oatcakes were sometimes called *bannocks*, meaning presents, or Noor cakes, meaning New Year's cakes, because they were the treats most often given out to children who came "begging" at Hogmanay or on the morning of New Year's Day. The children would perform in hopes of receiving Hogmanay oatcakes or fruit or pennies. They would wear large aprons which they could hold out to receive treats.

Arriving at a door, the children would announce:

> *Rise up, guidwife, an' shak' yer*
> *feathers,*
> *Dinna' think that we are beggars;*
> *We are guid folks come to play,*
> *Rise up an' gie's oor Hogmanay.*
> *Hogmanay, Trol-lol-lay.*

or:

> *Hogmanay, Trollolay,*
> *Give us your white bread and none*
> *of your grey.*

Finally, after all the parties, sports, visiting, feasting, and more, the official Hogmanay celebration comes to an end. It's not surprising that Scotland officially observes an extended New Year's Day holiday. Here, January 2 is a second national day off. It's time to rest up.

HIGHLAND HOLIDAY FUN AND GAMES

Christmas Day and New Year's Day are Scotland's two biggest sports days. Many kinds of ball games are played on these two days, and, in some places, everyone is expected to play.

Highlanders, famous for their love of games, are out in force these days. There are ball games, foot races, ice hockey, strength contests and mock battles, shooting matches, and toy boat sailing. In the past, cockfights were part of the fun. In Carglen in the late 1800's, schoolboys were expected to bring a gamecock to fight at the village school in the annual Hogmanay match.

Some ancient Christmas and New Year's holiday games such as shinty and kyles have been passed down through the generations.

In the Highlands, shinty, also called by its Gaelic name, *camanachd*, was played at midday on New Year's Day. Men in the area gathered at the selected field. A match between two villages or sides was chosen by two leaders from the same village.

When rival teams took the field on New Year's Day, everyone from the countryside turned out to play or watch and cheer their boys to victory.

Shinty was played by men or boys using curved sticks and a ball which was likely to be wooden, but could also be a ball of twisted hair, a cork, a knob from a tree trunk, or even a vertebrae from a sheep's backbone. The players tried to drive the ball to the hail, or goal, at either end of the playing field. The designated goals for a game were set from 100 yards to several miles apart.

The game started when the ball was either thrown up in the air between the two sides or buried in the ground to be dug up with the sticks. As soon as a team managed to drive the ball to their goal, the goals switched and they had to make their next score by driving it to the opposite end. With pipes playing, sticks flying, and a great crowd of men running and shouting, a game of shinty sometimes resembled a battle. When the game was called for darkness, there usually was a dinner and a dance.

In the ancient game of kyles, an iron ring was driven into the ground to stand upright. A player tried to roll an iron ball through the ring, or "kyle." Others stood alongside the game, throwing down coins and betting "a penny she kyles!" or "a penny she doesna'!" Often, nine-hole courses, like golf courses with rings instead of holes, were played.

In Aberdeenshire and other parts of northern Scotland, three days at Christmastime were focused on the local football, or "ba'in" game. Men gathered in the local churchyard for ba' matches, where "brute force, and not scientific skill, ruled the day and decided the issue of the fray."

In the Highlands, shinty has been played at midday on New Year's Day for many generations.

HOLIDAYS ON THE SCOTTISH ISLANDS

From grand old Viking centuries
Up-Helly-A' has come,
Then light the torch and form the march,
and sound the rolling drum:
And wake the mighty memories of heroes
that are dumb;
The waves are rolling on.

~ from "Up-Helly-A' Song,"
by J. J. Haldane Burgess and Thomas Manson

UP-HELLY-A'

The holiday season shines bright far off the north coast of Scotland long after it has ended everywhere else. In the Shetland Islands, Scotland's extreme northern reaches, the Christmas and New Year's holiday celebration closes with a real Viking-style blaze of glory called *Up-Helly-A'*.

The Shetland Islands lie north beyond the Orkney Islands, 110 miles out into the ocean from Scotland's mainland coast. A group of 100 small islands that spans 500 square miles, the Shetlands are as much Scandinavian as Scottish in their history. In fact, the islands were possessed by Norway from A.D. 875 until 1469 when King James III received

Each year, one Shetland islander is chosen as *Guiser Jarl*, the honorary leader of the Up-Helly-A' celebration. The Guiser Jarl represents a legendary ancient Viking for the event.

them as part of a dowry upon his marriage to Margaret, the daughter of King Christian I of Norway.

It's no surprise that Norse heritage remains a strong focus today. After all, the islands' biggest city, Lerwick, is closer to Bergen, the capital of Norway, than it is to Scotland's capital city, Edinburgh. From the unique Viking-inspired shape of their boats, to the design of their homes, to the unusual names of their villages and towns, the Shetlanders reflect pride in their Norse heritage. Never is this more clear than during the Christmas season.

The ancient Norse Yule festival that celebrated the return of the sun at the time of the winter solstice held strong sway over these northern island peoples. After all, winter is very long and very dark here, with the sun first appearing above the horizon after 9 a.m. and setting by 3 p.m. on winter's shortest days.

In Shetland, the Christmas season still is sometimes referred to as "Yule" or "the Yules," taking the ancient Norse name for the celebration. Yules, the plural, was used because it is a time of not one but several holiday festivals. The traditional 12 days of Christmas are just the first half of the fun here. In the Shetland Islands, the holiday season stretches 24 days.

The Up-Helly-A' celebration culminates with the ceremonial torching of a life-sized Viking galley.

Until World War I, this end-of-the-season celebration was held on January 12, New Year's Eve according to the old Julian calendar. Sometimes, however, the end of the holiday season was postponed for weeks, even into February. Today, the official Shetland Islands Up-Helly-A' celebration is regularly held in Lerwick, Shetland's largest town, on the last Tuesday of January each year.

A VIKING SEND-OFF

Up-Helly-A' translates as "the holiday is finished," and in the Shetlands, the season is given a real Viking send-off, with songs, flaming torches, and a conflagration engulfing a full-sized Viking galley.

Each year, in a top-secret selection process, one Shetlander is named to the esteemed post of *Guiser Jarl*, the honorary leader of the celebration. A *guiser* is the Scottish name for a person who dresses up in costume and travels about performing at the holidays. *Jarl* is a Norse word meaning "chieftain."

As the leader, the Up-Helly-A' Guiser Jarl represents a legendary ancient Viking for the event. Which great old Norseman the Guiser Jarl will play is kept a closely guarded secret. On Up-Helly-A' morning the Guiser Jarl and his "squad" of 50 or more men, dressed in full Viking gear, with dark-blue velvet *kirtles* (short coats), reindeer skin cloaks and boots, brass breast plates, helmets, axes, and swords, guide a 30-foot, ornately designed Viking galley, complete with carved dragon head, through the town to the harbor. There the galley remains on display while the Guiser Jarl and his squad visit schools, hospitals, and the town hall. At about 7:00 p.m., the Guiser Jarl leads a torchlight procession through the town. Altogether, over 900 guiser men, dressed in colorful and often outrageous outfits, carry torches, sing, and perform all along the route, as they make their way through the dark streets of town to the official burning site in a park near town hall.

Here, the marchers circle the galley, ringing it with their blazing torches. There are Viking songs, plus a silly song or two. Then, with three cheers for the galley builders and torch makers, for Up-Helly-A', and for the Jarl, all the guisers toss their torches into the Viking galley and watch it burn up in a spectacular ceremonial fire.

The Galley Song

Floats the ravan banner o'er us,
Round our Dragon Ship we stand,
Voices joined in gladsome chorus,
Raised aloft the flaming band.
Every guiser has a duty,
When he joins the festive throng,
Honour, freedom, love and beauty,
In the feast, the dance, the song.
Worthy sons of Vikings make us,
Truth be our encircling fire;
Shadowy visions backward take us,
To the Sea-King's fun'ral pyre.
Bonds of Brotherhood inherit,
O'er strife the curtain draw;
Let our actions breathe the spirit
Of our grand Up-Helly-A'.

WILD AND CRAZY GUISERS

While the old year and the holiday season have burned away with the galley, the fun of the evening in Lerwick is far from over. The more than 40 squads, or teams, of guisers make a cir-

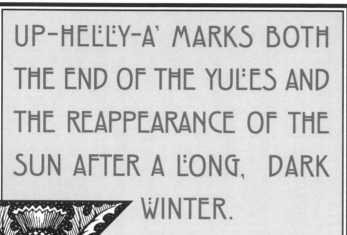

UP-HELLY-A' MARKS BOTH THE END OF THE YULES AND THE REAPPEARANCE OF THE SUN AFTER A LONG, DARK WINTER.

cuit of 11 local halls where townsfolk are waiting to be entertained.

Squads dress in crazy costumes and perform silly songs, skits, and dance routines to amuse their audiences. For their efforts, the guisers are rewarded at each stop with traditional hot spiced rum, plus other drinks and food. Then, it's off to the next venue.

HOW THE PARTY GOT STARTED

The Up-Helly-A' celebration with its burning galley is patterned after a pagan fire festival of the Vikings. This Viking-themed Shetland tradition, however, is actually a creation of modern times.

Lerwick's end-of-the-season festivities first kicked off in the early 1800's. This special night's first celebrants weren't

Vikings, but Scottish soldiers and sailors home from the Napoleonic Wars and looking for some rowdy fun. In 1824, a Methodist missionary visiting Lerwick noted:

"The whole town was in an uproar: from 12 o'clock last night until late this night blowing of horns, beating of drums, tinkling of old tin kettles, firing of guns, shouting, bawling, fiddling, fifing, drinking, fighting."

By 1840, blazing tar barrels had been added to the excitement. Rival groups carried lighted tar barrels through the streets, and meetings between groups sometimes were chaotic.

Finally, in the 1870's, the tar barrels were put aside and the rough and tumble fun was organized into today's Up-Helly-A', complete with torchlight procession, guising, and the Viking theme. In a few years, the Viking galley, the Guiser Jarl, and his squad of Vikings became part of the event.

Today, Up-Helly-A' draws visitors from all around the world.

HOLIDAY VISITORS

Up-Helly-A' marks the end of the Yules and the reappearance of the sun after a long, dark winter. Long ago, these darkest days of the year also were the time when the spirits of the dead were said to roam the earth.

In Orkney and the Shetlands, the dead always were welcome to rejoin the living and share in the Yule festivities. Houses and barns were cleaned and put in perfect order to look their best for returning relatives. Places were set for them at holiday tables. The dear departed were thought to bring good fortune to the people, homes, and livestock they visited.

In the more recent past, magical Yule visitors were more likely to be *trows*. Emerging from their underground world in the darkest days of mid-December, these nasty little fellows enjoyed wreaking havoc in the lives of people during the Yuletide season.

Many superstitions involved methods for keeping the troublesome trows at bay. The first line of defense was to make the sign of the cross over home, barns, and livestock. Also, crosses were hung over houses, over food, over everything.

Part of the enthusiasm in the Up-Helly-A' celebration at the end of the holidays was knowing that the fires on the last day of the holiday season will drive the terrible creatures back underground again until next year. In the past, at the stroke of midnight on this last day, Shetlanders would ceremoniously chase the trows out of their houses and back underground. Then, groups of young men would march from house to house with flaming torches to finish off any trows who might still linger.

ANCIENT STONES, ANCIENT SIGNS

The 67 islands and many islets which make up the Orkney Islands are filled

At Hogmanay, according to legend, the standing stones of the Orkney Islands, such as the Ring of Brodgar standing stones shown below, move about the land on their own. They return to their rightful positions before daylight.

with ancient ruins. More remains of old settlements are found here than anywhere else in Great Britain.

At Christmastime, legends and traditions swirl around Orkney's dozens of "standing stones." In the distant past, the northern Picts carved symbols all over the tall stones and placed them in position here and there for long forgotten reasons. At Hogmanay, according to legend, the standing stones move about the land on their own, returning to their rightful positions before daylight.

Five miles outside the town of Stromness in northeast Orkney is the Maes Howe mound, the most impressive chambered tomb found in Western Europe. Built 4,500 years ago as a tomb for a chieftain family, the 300-foot, several-roomed *cairn* was once surrounded by a moat. A more "recent" attraction at Maes Howe is the Viking graffiti left on its walls about 3,500 years ago.

At midwinter solstice, the sun shines directly into the southwest doorway of the mound and down a narrow 36-foot-long passage to shine brightly on the back wall of the tomb, lighting up its large inner chamber. This special feature carefully built into the tomb

Maes Howe, a mound in northeast Orkney built 4,500 years ago as a chieftain family tomb, was designed to mark the time of the winter solstice. At midwinter, the sun shines directly into the southwest doorway of the mound and down a narrow passage to shine brightly on the back wall of the tomb, lighting up its large inner chamber.

seems intended to mark not just the solstice itself, but a long period of celebration, almost a double month of days, surrounding that date.

Today, Maes Howe is a popular and very up-to-the-minute part of the midwinter holiday celebration in Scotland. A Maes Howe "cam" placed in the tomb goes live in early December each year, broadcasting the view inside the inner chamber over the Internet to anyone who wants to log on and share in the mystical experience from the comfort of their home computer. Site operators do remind viewers that it is December and it is Scotland, so don't expect the sun to put on a bright show every day.

ISLAND GAMES

Just as the Highlanders have their own holiday game traditions and events, so too, do Scotland's island areas.

In the Orkney Islands town of Stromness, up until the beginning of World War II, Christmas Eve was the time for an all-town tug of war. A tree—a rare commodity in the islands—was chained in the middle of the town's main street. Men from the north end of town battled men from the south end, each side trying to drag the tree to a goal in its own territory.

In Shetland days of auld, the tradition was for all the men and boys to join in a game of football which lasted as long as the fading light would allow.

On the island of Iona, every man, woman, and child old enough to swing a club will play a round of golf, regardless of the weather, on New Year's Day.

KIRKWALL'S BA' GAME

The most famous old sporting event of Christmas and New Year's is the ba' game, still played on these two days on the flagstoned streets of Kirkwall, the central city on Orkney's Mainland Island. Here, all the men in town join in a fierce match through the city streets between the "Uppies" and "Doonies" over control of the hard leather ba'.

Preparation for the Kirkwall Ba' game begins on Christmas Eve and New Year's Eve as shopkeepers and homeowners along the winding main streets of town secure their properties and erect barricades in front of windows and doors to shield against the melee to come.

For centuries, the two teams have been selected by where one lives. If you were born north of the St. Magnus Cathedral, you are a Doon-the-Gates, or Doonie. If you come from south of the cathedral, you're an Up-the-Gate, or Uppie. Now, many players join the team their fathers and grandfathers played for, regardless of their current addresses.

In the past, the game brought to the surface a very real rivalry between the Uppies and Doonies. Kirkwall was divided into an area to the south called the Laverock which was controlled by the Bishop and one to the north called the Burgh, which was controlled by the King's Earl. Until the mid-1900's, the feud was so intense that Uppies and Doonies were careful to stay out of each other's territory throughout the year.

The object of the game is to move the ba', a hard, cork-filled leather ball

forward until it reaches the goal and sudden victory. The Uppies strive to touch the ba' against a wall in the south end of town. The Doonies want to drive the ba' to the north and into the harbor water.

The Christmas Day or New Year's Day action begins at 1 p.m. Partici-

The Uppies and Doonies meet on Christmas and New Year's Day in front of the Mercat Cross in Kirkwall, Orkney's Mainland Island to play the ba' game that has made the teams rivals for centuries. The ba' is a hard, 3-pound, cork-filled leather ball. When the St. Magnus Cathedral bells chime, a local official or an admired former player throws up the ba' and 200 or more men push forward to take control.

pants gather at Broad Street in front of the Mercat Cross on the Kirk Green opposite St. Magnus Cathedral. When the cathedral bells chime, a local official or an admired former player throws up the ba' and 200 or more men push forward to take control. The throng around the ball packs the street, making it nearly impossible to move in any direction at first, and difficult even to find the ba'.

A ba' game can last for hours, the scrimmage pushing great distances back and forth, up and down the street before a goal is reached. The game is wild and fast; the rules are vague at best. Players in possession of the ball have been known to sneak down alleys and climb over rooftops to escape the opposition. While the action is rough, foul play and poor sportsmanship are strictly out. In the past, the game was like Scottish football, with only kicking allowed to move the ball. Today's game is much more free-wheeling and kicking is only part of the action.

The cork-filled, leather 3-pound ba' itself is a work of art, carefully handmade by local craftsmen. The leather case is hand stitched. The stitching alone can take as long as two days to complete. Then the ba' is painted in alternating black and natural-colored panels. The cork dust center helps to make the ba' hard. It also ensures that it will float should the ba' end up in the harbor. This "modern" ba' was designed over 150 years ago. The original ba' was simply an inflated animal bladder reinforced with leather.

As a warm-up to the men's game, a boys ba' game is played at 10:30 a.m.

on Christmas and New Year's Day. In 1945 and 1946, 20 to 30 women hit the streets for their own ba' game. When the first 90-minute battle between Uppie and Doonie women ended, an appropriately named Uppie, Margaret Yule, took the ba' trophy as most valuable player on the winning side. Men opposed women taking on the sport, and the women's version was quickly stopped. But Scottish women are talking about starting up their own game again.

The Christmas and New Year's Day ba' games have been played in their present form faithfully since 1850. However, the action started long before that, with the ancient Scottish Yule tradition of mass football games during the holidays. Such games were a main feature of the holidays throughout the region for hundreds of years.

Some say the Orkney Island game represents the new year battling with the old. However, there is a remarkable legend associated with the ba' game's origin.

According to the tale, a young man of the islands crossed to the mainland and defeated an evil tyrant named Tusker. The boy cut off the tyrant's head, tied it to his saddle, and headed back to Orkney. As the young boy galloped along, a tooth of the bouncing severed head punctured his leg, causing an infection. The boy reached the Mercat Cross, tossed the head into the gathered crowd, and died. Angered at the boy's death, the townsfolk kicked the head through the streets of town.

This story is not true, but is based on a similar one which is true. The Orkney

Earl Sigurd really did travel to the mainland to defeat his enemy Maelbrigte Tusk. He and his men tied their enemies' severed heads to their saddles after the battle. As he was riding, Sigurd's leg was punctured by a tooth on Maelbrigte's head. Sigurd died and was buried on the mainland.

A tamer idea ties the ba' game to ancient agrarian rites. Supposedly, a ba' pushed up through town brought a good harvest in the year ahead. A ba' driven into the harbor would bring bountiful fishing.

An old rhyme describes an Uppie victory:

Up wi' the Ba' boys,
Up wi' the Ba',
An' ye'll get cheap meal,
An' tatties an' a'.

HANDSEL MONDAY

Handsel Monday's drawin' near,
Ale and shortbread will appear.

Handsel Monday, which falls on the first Monday after New Year's Day, rounds out the traditional Christmas season. Depending on whether you follow the new or auld calendar, Handsel Monday could land anywhere from January 8 to January 19. Whenever it came, Handsel Monday was a most welcome day for the working class.

A handsel is a gift and Handsel Monday was the day for remembering servants, postmen, newspaper deliverers, and other workers who perform personal services, as well as tenants, with money or presents. Unlike the friendly gifts freely offered at Hogmanay, a handsel is something expected, a bonus that is a traditional part of the yearly wage. In some places, this custom even included children being expected to give money to their schoolteachers.

For working class people, Handsel Monday, unlike Christmas, was the one true, guaranteed day off and a day for receiving gifts and food. The party today was even better than Hogmanay for many because now there was money to spend and free time to spend it. This free day was also a popular wedding day for workers.

Soon after midnight, before Handsel Monday, the celebration began with flaming torches and music and merrymaking in the streets. Then, when day came, there were lavish meals provided by masters and employers. This was the time for the handsels to be given out. On the morning of Handsel Monday, it was considered lucky to stay in bed awhile, both because you didn't have to work and because fairies and witches were out and about.

Having finally been given a day off, many times workers found it hard to stop celebrating. Handsel Monday sometimes stretched into Handsel Tuesday, and even to a whole week of fun. Now, all the New Year's games were back in full force.

Handsel Monday was eventually blended into Hogmanay, adding its fuel to the grand Scottish New Year's celebration.

TWELFTH NIGHT

Twelfth Night, or Epiphany, commemorates the arrival of the Three Wise Men at the stable in Bethlehem. This holiday is celebrated on January 6, where it falls according to the Gregorian calendar. Until 1660, Twelfth Night was celebrated in Scotland on January 12, the "auld" Julian calendar date. In some parts of the Highlands and islands, January 12 still holds sway as the proper night to celebrate. Twelfth Night is celebrated beginning on the eve of the holiday itself.

In keeping with the character of the old "Daft Days" of the Christmas season, the eve of Twelfth Night is all about the fun of "misrule" and turning established order on its head. In the past, Twelfth Night was called *Uphalieday* in Scotland. Like the Up-Helly-A' name given to the end-of-season celebration in the Shetland Islands, Uphalieday translates literally as "the holiday is finished."

Uphalieday originally was an all-night party, complete with dancing, singing, feasting, guising, and silliness.

To chose rulers for this night, a rich cake was baked with a bean and a pea inside. The man who found the bean in his piece was king for a night. The woman who found the pea became queen. These one-night monarchs could command dinner companions to dance, sing, and perform for their amusement.

This pauper-becomes-prince fun even was enjoyed by the

Scotland's beloved black bun cake is a Twelfth Night tradition. A coin is baked inside that brings luck in the year ahead to its discoverer.

country's royalty. In 1563, the English ambassador to Edinburgh decribed the events at court on Twelfth Night when Mary Queen of Scots gave her crown to two of her ladies-in-waiting for the night and even dressed them in her own robes and jewels:

"The Queen of the Bean was that day in a gown of cloth of silver, her head, her neck, her shoulders, the rest of her whole body, so beset with stones, that more in our whole jewel house were not to be found."

Today, Scotland's beloved black bun is part of this tradition. A coin is baked inside which brings luck in the year ahead to its discoverer.

Twelfth Night is a last all-out party night before the world gets back to business as usual. A Scottish Twelfth Night party always ends with taking down the holiday decorations. This is because all the good luck, health, fertility, and protection from witches provided by the greenery draped around the house throughout the holidays will be broken if decorations stay up past Twelfth Night.

In the past, Plough Monday, the first Monday after Twelfth Night, was time for all work, including plowing the fields, to begin again. But first, young men dressed in wild costumes dragged a plow around the village, playing music and demanding money. If you gave money, you got a hearty cheer. If you did not, you might hear, "Hunger and starvation to you!" and wake up the next morning to find an unwanted furrow in your yard.

SCOTTISH CRAFTS

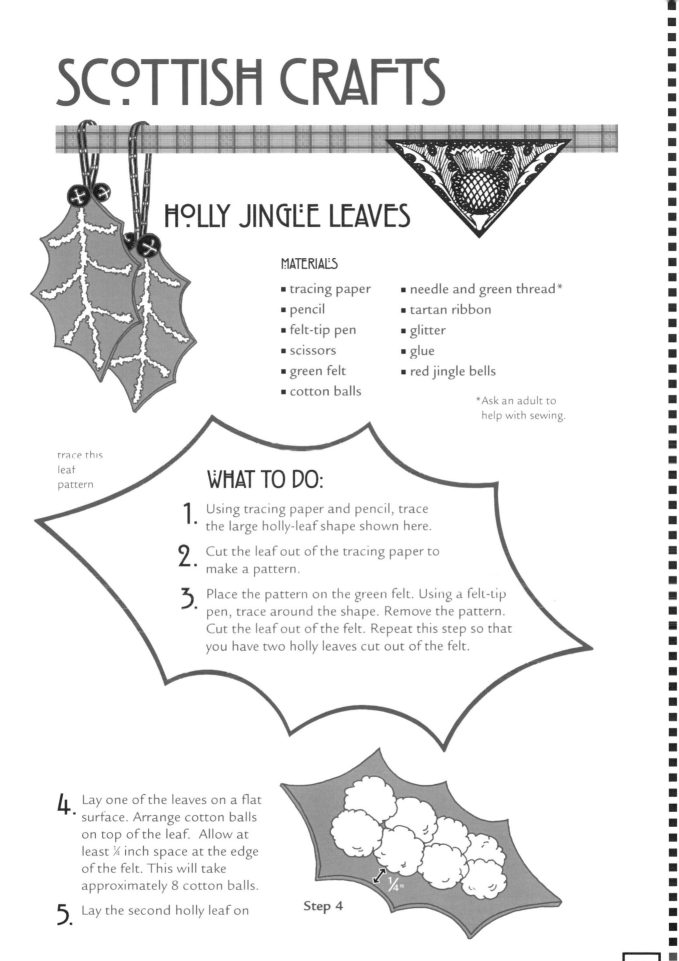

HOLLY JINGLE LEAVES

MATERIALS

- tracing paper
- pencil
- felt-tip pen
- scissors
- green felt
- cotton balls
- needle and green thread*
- tartan ribbon
- glitter
- glue
- red jingle bells

*Ask an adult to help with sewing.

trace this leaf pattern

WHAT TO DO:

1. Using tracing paper and pencil, trace the large holly-leaf shape shown here.

2. Cut the leaf out of the tracing paper to make a pattern.

3. Place the pattern on the green felt. Using a felt-tip pen, trace around the shape. Remove the pattern. Cut the leaf out of the felt. Repeat this step so that you have two holly leaves cut out of the felt.

4. Lay one of the leaves on a flat surface. Arrange cotton balls on top of the leaf. Allow at least ¼ inch space at the edge of the felt. This will take approximately 8 cotton balls.

5. Lay the second holly leaf on

¼"

Step 4

top of the cotton-ball layer. Carefully pick up the leaf bundle and sew around the edges.* Sew around the edges a second time to secure.

6. When you have finished

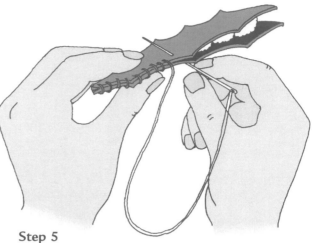

Step 5

sewing around the edges, use the tartan ribbon to make a loop hanger. Cut 4 inches of ribbon, make a loop and sew the edges to the leaf.

7. Decorate your holly leaf by drawing vein lines in glue and sprinkling them with glitter. Let the glue dry thoroughly before you proceed to the next step.

8. Finish the holly leaf by sewing on two or three red jingle bells to look like red holly berries.* To hide the edges of the ribbon hanger, place the jingle bells over the edges.

9. Hang your holly jingle

Step 8

leaf on your Christmas tree or in a window. You can even use it to decorate a package. In that case, instead of gluing glitter veins on the leaf, write the name of the recipient in glue on the leaf and then sprinkle with glitter. When the glue has dried, thread ribbon through the hanger and tie it onto the package with a bow.

HOLLY JINGLE BERRY WREATH

Note: Children under the age of 10 should not use the glue gun alone.

MATERIALS

- 12-inch green styrofoam wreath
- holly jingle leaves, see page 65*
- hot-glue gun
- red tartan ribbon
- red jingle bells
- string to form a hanger

*you will need a yard of green felt to make the 17 holly jingle leaves that make up the wreath

WHAT TO DO:

1. Make 17 holly jingle leaves, see page 65. Follow steps 1 through 5 and 7. Do not make a ribbon hanger for the leaves and do not sew on the red jingle bells.

2. Using the hot-glue gun, glue 11 leaves around the outside of the styrofoam wreath, as shown in the illustration.

3. To attach the inside circle of leaves, lift up one of the outer leaves and tuck under the tip of the leaf. Using the hot-glue gun, attach the leaf into position on the styrofoam wreath. Repeat with the remaining 5 leaves.

4. Tie a red tartan ribbon bow around the top of the wreath.

5. To form a hanger for the wreath, tie a piece of string around the back of the ribbon. Leave enough string to form a loop.

6. Using the hot-glue gun, glue the red jingle bells around the wreath in groups of three.

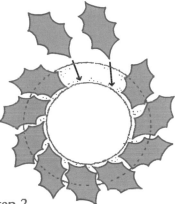

Step 2

Step 3

FLUFFY LAMB ORNAMENT

MATERIALS

- pencil
- tracing paper
- scissors
- white construction paper
- black pipe cleaners
- green ribbon
- glue
- 8-inch piece of white ribbon
- cotton balls
- 2 gold, silver, or white sequins
- spray glue
- clear or silver glitter
- red tartan ribbon

WHAT TO DO:

1. Using tracing paper, trace the oval shape on this page and cut out your tracing. Then trace your pattern onto a sheet of white construction paper. Cut the oval out of the paper. This will be the lamb's body.

2. Cut two 3-inch lengths of the pipe cleaner. Bend both of these in half and glue to the bottom of the oval. These will become the legs for the lamb.

3. Wind one pipe cleaner into an oval shape. This will become one side of the head of the lamb. Be sure to leave a bit of it unwound at the end as shown. Glue the end of the pipe cleaner onto the white construction paper body.

trace this oval as the pattern for the lamb's body

Step 3

4. To make the ears, cut two ¾-inch lengths of pipe cleaner and bend in half. Glue these two pieces side by side to the back of the oval head you just glued in step 3.

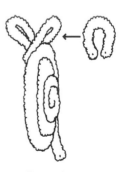

Step 4

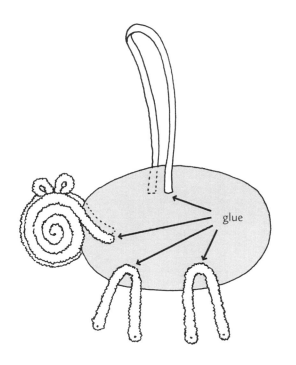

5. Repeat step 3 to form the other side of the lamb's head. Glue it to the back of the head you made in step 3. Be sure to add some glue to the end that rests on the construction paper.

6. Make a hanger for your ornament by cutting an 8-inch piece of white ribbon. Fold this in half and glue one end on each side of the top of the construction-paper body.

7. When the glue has dried, it is time to put on the lamb's fluffy coat. Start by gluing cotton balls onto the construction-paper body. Place the cotton balls close to each other so that none of the construction paper is showing. The cotton balls should overlap the outside edge of the construction paper and cover up the edges of pipe cleaner that you glued onto the construction paper.

8. Glue two more cotton balls to the center of the lamb's body to add a second layer. This will make the lamb look very fluffy.

9. When the glue on the cotton balls has dried, repeat steps 7 and 8 on the other side.

10. Give the lamb eyes by gluing one sequin to each side of the head.

11. Before you use the spray glue, cover the lamb's head and legs with a tissue so that the glue will stick only to the cotton balls. Spray-glue one side of the lamb's body and sprinkle with glitter. Repeat this step for the other side.

12. When the spray glue has dried, finish your lamb ornament by tying a tartan bow around the lamb's neck to hang on your Christmas tree.

HOLIDAY CANDLE HOLDER

MATERIALS

- air-drying clay*
- candle**
- holiday decorations, such as artificial evergreen branches, artificial holly berries, small ornaments
- ribbon

*available at arts and crafts stores

**Do not light candle without an adult present.

WHAT TO DO:

1. Using the air-drying clay, make a ball that is approximately 2½ inches in diameter. Flatten one end of the ball and insert the candle in the other. The candle should be inserted more than halfway into the ball. Be sure the ball can sit firmly on a tabletop.

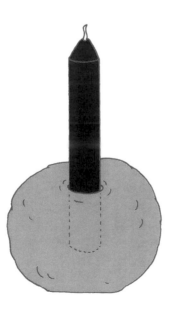

2. Before the clay dries, stick the artificial holiday decorations into the ball, on top, around the candle. Follow the instructions on the package for drying time of the clay.

3. Finish your candle holder by wrapping a ribbon around the base of the ball.

SCOTTISH CAROLS

AULD LANG SYNE

Words by Robert Burns
Music: Traditional

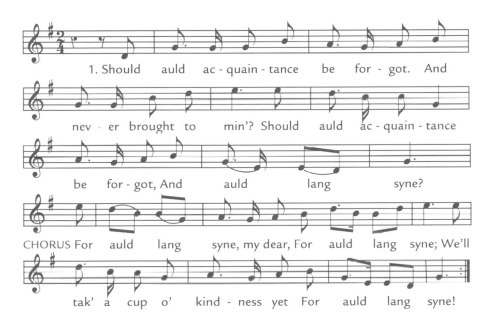

1. Should auld ac-quain-tance be for-got. And nev-er brought to min'? Should auld ac-quain-tance be for-got, And auld lang syne?

CHORUS For auld lang syne, my dear, For auld lang syne; We'll tak' a cup o' kind-ness yet For auld lang syne!

And surely ye'll be your pint-stowp,
And surely I'll be mine,
And we'll tak' a cup o' kindness yet
For auld lang syne!

[CHORUS]

We twa hae run about the braes,
And pou'd the gowans fine,
But we've wander'd monie a weary fit
Sin' auld lang syne.

[CHORUS]

We twa hae paidl'd in the burn
Frae morning sun till dine,
But seas between us braid hae roar'd
Sin' auld lang syne.

[CHORUS]

And there's a hand, my trusty fiere,
And gie's a hand o' thine,
And we'll tak' a richt guid-willie waught
For auld lang syne!

[CHORUS]

A GUID NEW YEAR

Words by Peter Livingstone
Music by Alex Hume

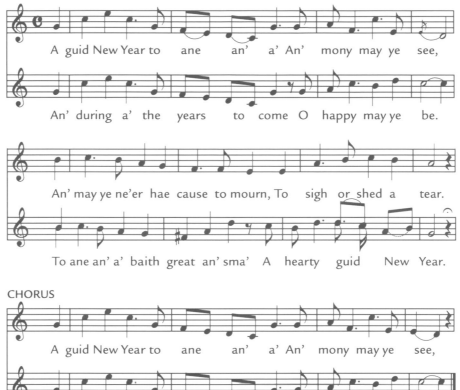

A guid New Year to ane an' a' An' mony may ye see,

An' during a' the years to come O happy may ye be.

An' may ye ne'er hae cause to mourn, To sigh or shed a tear.

To ane an' a' baith great an' sma' A hearty guid New Year.

CHORUS

A guid New Year to ane an' a' An' mony may ye see,

An' during a' the years to come O happy may ye be.

Oh time flies past, he winna wait,
My friend for you or me,
He works his wonders day by day
And onward still doth flee.
O wha can tell when ilka ane
I see sae happy here
Will meet again and merry be
Anither guid New Year.

[CHORUS]

We twa ha'e baith been happy lang.
We ran about the braes.
In yon wee cot beneath the tree
We spent our early days.
We ran about the burnie's side

The spot will aye be dear,
An' those that used to meet us there
We'll think on mony a year.

[CHORUS]

Noo let us hope our years may be
As guid as they ha'e been,
And trust we ne'er again may see
The sorrows we ha'e seen.
And let us wish that ane an' a'
Our friends baith far an' near
May aye enjoy in times to come
A hearty guid New Year.

[CHORUS]

SCOTTISH RECIPES

HAGGIS

2 lb. oatmeal (not instant)
1 lb. calf, pig, or lamb liver
1 large onion
1 lb. beef suet

½ tsp. cayenne pepper
½ tsp. ground allspice
½ tsp. salt
½ tsp. pepper

Put the oatmeal on a baking sheet and place the sheet under the broiler until the oatmeal turns lightly brown and crisp. Put the liver and onion in a large saucepan and pour in enough water to cover. Cook over medium-high heat for about 30 minutes. Drain the liver and onion, reserving 2 cups of the stock. Chop up the liver and onion. In a large bowl, combine the oatmeal, liver, onions, reserved stock, suet, and spices and mix well. Put the mixture into a 2-lb. clean coffee can or two 1-lb. cans. Bring a large pot of water to a boil. Carefully lower the can or cans inside the boiling water. Simmer uncovered for about 3 hours, replacing the water in the pan when needed.

Makes 6 to 8 servings.

ROAST GOOSE

1 10-lb. goose
½ head chopped garlic

1 tsp. salt
½ tsp. black pepper

Preheat the oven to 450 °F. Clean the goose, rub it with the garlic, then sprinkle with salt and pepper. Fill the goose with stuffing (recipe below) or cook the dressing separately. Place the goose on a rack in an uncovered roasting pan. Cook for 5 hours, basting frequently, allowing the goose to brown well.

Dressing for Goose:

2 cups cornbread crumbs
2 cups day-old crustless
    white bread, cubed
1 cup chopped celery

2 eggs
1 medium onion, chopped
1 tsp. basil
¾ tsp. salt

½ tsp. paprika
⅛ tsp. nutmeg
¼ cup fresh chopped parsley
chicken broth

In a large mixing bowl, combine all the ingredients except the chicken broth. Add only enough broth to moisten the stuffing. Stuff the goose with dressing or cook the dressing in a separate saucepan until warm.

Makes 10 servings.

COCK-A-LEEKIE SOUP

4 cups water
2 chicken bouillon cubes
1 lb. leeks, trimmed
  and sliced
2 ½ lbs. fresh whole chicken

salt and pepper to taste
¼ cup fresh parsley,
  chopped
1 bay leaf
1 tsp. dried thyme

12 prunes soaked
  overnight (optional)
1 tbsp. cornstarch
  mixed with 2 tbsp. water
chopped parsley to garnish

In a large saucepan, bring the water to a boil. Add the bouillon cubes and stir until they dissolve. Add the leeks, chicken, salt, pepper, parsley, bay leaf, and thyme. Turn the heat to low and simmer gently for 1 to 1 ½ hours, until the chicken is tender.

Remove the chicken from the pan, skin it, and cut the meat into bite-sized pieces. Return the chicken to the pan. Add the prunes, if desired. Simmer for 20 minutes.

Thicken the soup with the cornstarch and water mixture. Stir in the parsley. The soup tastes better if made a day in advance.

Makes 8 to 10 servings.

STEAK AND KIDNEY PIE

Filling:

1 cup flour
1 tsp. salt
¼ tsp. pepper
⅛ tsp. nutmeg
1 ½ lbs. round steak
¾ lb. veal or lamb kidneys

3 tbsp. butter
1 medium onion,
  chopped
1 14-oz. can beef broth
1 cup dry red wine

Pastry:

2 cups flour
½ tsp. salt
1 stick butter
6 tbsp. cold water

Preheat the oven to 350 °F. In a plastic storage bag, combine the flour, salt, pepper, and nutmeg. Shake to mix. Slice the steak ½-inch thick. Put the steak into the bag of seasoned flour and shake to coat; set aside. Slice the kidney ½-inch thick. Melt the butter in a large frying pan over high heat. Add the kidneys and sauté for 1 to 2 minutes, stirring constantly. Add the onions, turn the heat to medium, and sauté until the onions are soft and transparent. Coat a casserole dish with cooking spray, then place a layer of meat, then a layer of kidneys and onions in the dish. Pour the beef broth and wine over the meats. Cover the dish and bake for 1 to 1 ½ hours.

Meanwhile, prepare the pastry. Sift together the flour and salt. With your fingers, work in the butter until you have a coarse mixture. Add the water and mix to form an elastic dough.

Put the dough in the refrigerator until you need it.

Remove the steak and kidney pie from the oven and allow to cool slightly. Roll out the dough large enough to cover the pie. Cover the meat with the pastry. Bake 12 to 15 minutes.

Makes 6 servings.

VENISON STEW

1 lb. venison
1 lb. bacon
2 tbsp. butter
salt and pepper
1 lb. carrots, sliced

½ cup celery, chopped
1 large onion, sliced
1 tbsp. orange peel, grated
1 ¼ cups milk
1 tsp. dried thyme

1 tbsp. cornstarch mixed
  with 2 tbsp. water
2 tbsp. whiskey
½ cup heavy cream

Cut venison into strips. Melt the butter in a skillet over medium high heat. Add the venison strips and bacon and brown the two meats. Add the salt and pepper to taste. Stir in the sliced carrots, chopped celery, sliced onion, and grated orange peel. Pour in the milk and add the thyme. Cover, reduce the heat, and simmer for 2 hours, until the venison is tender.

Remove the meat and vegetables with a slotted spoon. Add the cornstarch and water mixture to thicken the juice. Then add the whiskey and cream. Heat gently until thick and smooth. Add the meat back to the pan and stir to mix the meat and gravy.

Serves 6 to 8.

BLACK BUN

Casing:

½ cup (1 stick) butter
2 cups flour
½ tsp. baking powder
4 tbsp. cold water
1 egg, beaten

Filling:

2 lbs. seedless raisins
3 lbs. currants
½ lb. blanched
  almonds, chopped
3 cups white flour
1 cup granulated sugar
2 tsp. allspice

1 tsp. ground ginger
1 tsp. cinnamon
¼ tsp. black pepper
1 tsp. cream of tartar
1 tsp. baking powder
1 tbsp. brandy
½ cup milk

Preheat the oven to 225 °F. To prepare the casing, cut the butter into the flour using a pastry knife. Add the baking powder and cold water and mix to a stiff paste. Put the mixture onto a floured surface and roll out to thin sheet. Grease an 8-inch-square baking pan. Line the pan with the casing, pinching off enough to make a top crust.

For the filling, in a large bowl combine all the ingredients, except the milk. Add just enough milk to moisten the mixture. Put the mixture into the pastry-lined pan. Cover with remaining pastry; dampen the edges so the top and bottom pastries stick together. Prick all over the top pastry with a fork. Brush with beaten egg. Cook for 3 hours. Store the black bun in an airtight tin.

Makes 8 to 10 servings.

DUNDEE CAKE

1 cup mixed citrus fruit peel, chopped
1 cup seedless raisins
1 cup currants
1 cup glacé cherries, cut in half
⅔ cup butter
⅔ cup sugar
4 eggs
2 cups flour
1 tbsp. ground almonds
juice and grated rind of ½ lemon
pinch of salt
1 tsp. baking powder
1 tbsp. brandy or rum
1 oz. blanched split almonds
2 tbsp. milk mixed with 1 tbsp. sugar

Preheat the oven to 225 °F. Place the mixed peel, raisins, currants, and glacé cherries in a 2-quart casserole dish. Mix thoroughly with the hands, cover, and bake for 20 minutes, or until the mixture is sticky and completely heated, stirring at least once with a fork. Remove fruit mixture from oven and allow to cool completely before using. Turn up the oven to 300 °F.

In a large mixing bowl, cream together the butter and sugar. Add one egg and ¼ cup of flour, beat well, and then repeat until all four eggs and all the flour has been added. Stir in the ground almonds, baked fruit mixture, lemon rind and juice, and salt. Add the baking powder and brandy or rum and stir to mix.

Pour the batter into a greased 8-inch square baking pan lined with wax paper. Cover the pan with foil and bake at 300 °F for 2 ½ hours. Halfway through cooking, remove the foil, scatter the split almonds on top, and then return to the oven. About 5 minutes before the cake is done, brush the top with the sugared milk. Return the cake to the oven. When the milk and sugar has dried to form a glaze, remove the cake from the oven. Allow cake to cool completely in the pan. Cut into squares.

Makes 9 servings.

GLOSSARY

Atholl brose (ATH uhl brohz) - a sweet Hogmanay drink made of oatmeal mixed with whiskey, cream, honey, and eggs.

ba' (baw) - a hard, 3-pound, cork-filled leather ball used in a traditional Scottish ball game played in Kirkwall, Orkney, on New Year's Day.

bannock (BAN uhk) - a flat, round or oval cake, usually unleavened, made of oatmeal or barley flour. Scottish children "beg" for bannocks on Hogmanay or on the morning of New Year's Day.

cailleach (KAYL yuhk) - the gaelic name for the spirit of "Old Winter"; it also means an old woman or nun.

camanachd (KA mahn ahkh) - the gaelic name for shinty, a ball game played in the Scottish Highlands.

ceilidh (KAY lee) - a traditional Scottish dance; also an informal social gathering for storytelling and especially singing.

clootie dumpling (KLOO tee DUHM plihng) - a sweet cake with raisins and spices that is boiled in a cloth. Clootie dumpling is a traditional Hogmanay and New Year's Day dessert in Scotland.

Flambeaux (FLAM boh) - tall torches that are lit by people of Comrie during Hogmanay celebration.

grulik (GROO lihk) - a costumed caroler in the Shetland Islands. Groups of gruliks go door-to-door wearing large white shirts covered with straw and white cloths covering their faces. Also called *skeklers* (SKEHK luhrz).

guiser (GYZ ur) - a person who wears a disguise. A guiser is the Scottish name for a person who dresses up in costume and travels about performing at the holidays.

Guiser Jarl (GYZ ur yarl) - the honorary leader of the Up-Helly-A' celebration. The Guiser Jarl represents a legendary ancient Viking for the event. *Jarl* is the Norse word for chieftain.

haggis (HAG is) - famous Scottish pudding made from the heart, lungs, and liver of a sheep or calf, chopped up and then mixed with suet, oatmeal, onions, and seasonings and boiled in the stomach of the animal. Haggis is traditionally served on Christmas or New Year's Day in Scotland.

handsel (HAN suhl) - a gift made as a token of good wishes at New Year's.

het pint (heht pynt) - a steaming, spiced mulled ale served at New Year in Scotland. Het pint is traditionally carried by first-footers in a copper kettle on Hogmanay.

Hogmanay (HAWG muh NAY) - New Year's Eve in Scotland, often celebrated with fireworks, parties, gifts, and calling at friends' homes.

Maes Howe (mayz how) - a mound in northeast Orkney, built 4,500 years ago as a tomb, which marks the time of the winter solstice.

neeps (neeps) **and nips** (nihps) - Scottish for mashed turnips and whiskey, customarily served with haggis on Christmas or New Year's Day in Scotland.

neeps (neeps) **and tatties** (TAHT eez) - Scottish for mashed turnips and potatoes, part of a traditional Scottish Christmas dinner.

Ne'er's Day (NAYRZ day) - Scottish for New Year's Day.

Nollaig Beag (NAHL ehk bayk) - Celtic for "little Christmas"; New Year's Day is sometimes called Nollaig Beag in Scotland.

Nollaig Mhor (NAHL ehk mohr) - Celtic for "big Christmas"; Christmas is sometimes called Nollaig Mhor in Scotland.

Oidche Choinnle (UH ee kuh KOY luh) - Celtic for "night of the candles." Christmas Eve and New Year's Eve in the Highlands and Scottish Islands are sometimes called Oidhche Chaluinne because Scottish families place candles in their windows.

sowens (SOH uhnz) - a porridge made from the fermented inner husks of oats. Served at Christmas in Scotland with honey, black treacle, and whiskey.

thigging (THIHG ing) - begging for gifts to help the needy on New Year's Day.

Up-Helly-A' (UHP hehl ee AH) - a celebration which takes place in Lerwick, in the Shetland Islands, on the last Tuesday in January, and reenacts the Nordic celebration of the triumph of the sun over the darkness of winter. The celebration includes a torchlit procession and the burning of a replica of a Viking galley. Translates as "the holiday is finished."

Uphalieday (uhp HAL ee day) - Scots term for Twelfth Night, or Epiphany, celebrated on January 6.

INDEX

Page numbers in *italic* type refer to illustrations.

A

Aberdeen, 38, 53
Agricola, Gnaeus Julius, 8
Alba, 9
Animals, 33, 36, 42-43
Atholl brose, 30-31, 39
"Auld Farmer's New Year Morning Salutation, The" (Burns), 42
"Auld Lang Syne" (song), *37*, 38, 39, 48, 71

B

Ba' game, 61-63
Balder, 16
Ball games, 53, 61-63
Bannocks, 52
Beaker folk, 8
Bees, 42
Begging, 52
Biggar, 15, 18-19
Birds, 42
Black bun, 30, 33, 38, 64, 75
Borthwick Castle, *20*
Boxing Day, 26
Bread, 29-30. *See also* **Shortbread**
Burghead, 15, 19
Burns, Robert, 38, 42

C

Cailleach, 10
Cakes, 29-31, 33, 38, 43, 64, 75
Caledonia, 8
Camanchd. *See* **Shinty**
Candlemas Bull, 43
Candles, 26-27, 36, 70
Caroling, 37. *See also* **Songs**
Cats, 43
Ceilidh dances, 46
Celts, 8-9, 17, 21, 24, 34
  festivals, 12, 15, 18
  mistletoe customs, 16
Charles I of England, 23-24
Charles II of England, 24
Children's customs, 27-28, 52
Christianity, 9, 14, 22
Christmas. *See also* **Yule**
  animals, 42-43

banned in Scotland, 7, 9, 23-26
before ban, 21-23
children's customs, 27-28
decorations, 26-27
food, 28-31
guising, 40-41
on islands, 56, 60-62
revived in Scotland, 26
sports, 53, 60-62
Christmas crackers, *30*
Christmas trees, 24
Clavie, Burning of the, 15, 19
Clootie dumpling, 38
Cock-a-leekie soup, 74
Columba, Saint, 9
Comrie, 15, 19
Crafts, 65-70
Creaming the well, 10-11
Cromwell, Oliver, 24

D

Daft Days, 22-23, 64
Dances, 46
Death, 11
Devilment, 51-52
Dies Natalis Solis Invicta, 14
Doonies, 61-63
Dram, 32, 33, 39
Drink, 30-33, 38-39
Druids, 12, 15-16, 19, 24, 27
Dundee, 32, 38, 49, 51
Dundee cake, 30, 75

E

Edinburgh, 23, 24, 51
  Hogmanay celebration, 7, 33, *35*, 37, 45-48, 50
Edinburgh Castle, 47, 48, 50
Elizabeth I of England, 23
England, 9, 21-24
Epiphany. *See* **Twelfth Night**
Etive, Loch, *43*
European Union, 45

F

Feast of St. Stephen, 26
Fife (region), 36-37

Fire
  household, 10, 11, 36
  in festivities, 12, 14-15, 18-19, 47-48, 57, 59
First-footers, 27, 32-33, 37-39
Firth of Forth, 51
Fishing, 43
Flag of Scotland, *9*
Flambeaux, Lighting of the, 15, 19
Food, 28-31, 38-39, 63, 73-76. *See also* **Cakes**
Football, 53, 60, 62
Fortunetelling, 10-11, 32, 33, 42-43
Freya, 15
Frigg, 16

G

Galley Song, 57
Gifts, 11, 17, *27*, 32, 37, 63
Ginger wine, 39
Glasgow, *6*, 33, 38
  Hogmanay celebration, 33, 38, 45, 46, 48-49
Golf, 60
Good luck. *See* **Fortunetelling**
Greenery, 15-17, 26-27
Grulicks, 40
"Guid New Year, A" (song), 34, 72
Guiser Jarl, *55*, 57-58
Guisers, 22-23, 40-41, 57-58

H

Haggis, 29, 73
Handsel Monday, 63
Het pint, 32, 38-39
Highlands, 36, 53
Hogmanay. *See also* **New Year's Eve**
  animals, 42-43
  bonfires, 18-19
  celebrating, 36-41
  feasting, 29-30, 38-39
  first-footing, 27, 32-33, 37-39
  in various cities, 45-50

origins, 7-9, 25-26, 41
preparations, 34-36
toasts, 10
Hogmanay Hooley, 49
Hogmanay lads, 40
Holly, 15-16, 27, 65-67

I

Internet, 50, 60
Inverness, 45, 49
Islands, Scottish, 36, 40, 54-63

J

James I of England, 23
James VI of Scotland. *See*
James I of England
Juniper, 15, 27

K

Kirkwall, *25*, 61-63
Knox, John, 9, 23
Kyles, 53

L

Lanark, 33
"Lang may your lum reek"
(toast), 10
Lerwick, 56-58
Linlithgow Loch, *12*
Loki, 16
Lomond, Loch, *2*
Loony Dook, 51

M

MacAlpin, Kenneth , 9
Maelbrigte Tusk, 63
Maes Howe mound, 60
Malcolm III of Scotland, 21 22
Margaret of Scotland, St., 21-
22
Mary, Queen of Scots, 23, 47,
64
Mercat Cross, *61, 62*
Mistletoe, 15-17, 27
Mummers. *See* Guisers
Music. *See* Caroling; Dances

N

National Covenant, 23-24
Neeps and nips, 29
Neeps and tatties, 29
Ne'er's Day. *See* New Year's
Day

Ne'er's Day Dook, 51
Ne'er's Eve. *See* New Year's
Eve
"Nemo Me Impune Lacessit"
(motto), 9
New Year's Day
begging, 52
Celtic, 21
devilment, 51-52
festivities, 50-51
fortunetelling, 10-11, 42-43
on islands, 57, 60
sports, 53, 61-62
New Year's Eve, 7, 10, 61. *See
also* Hogmanay
Nollaig Beag, 21
Nollaig Mhor, 21
Norsemen. *See* Vikings

O

Oatcakes, 30-31, 33, 38, 43,
52
Oban, Argyll, *50*
Odin, 16, 17, 27
Oidhche Chaluinne, 36
Orkney Islands, 54, 58-63

P

Paganism, 12-15, 24
Picts, 8-9, 60
Plough Monday, 64
Prayers, 31
Protestantism, 9, 23, 24
Pudding, Christmas, 28

R

Recipes, 73-76
Reformation, 9, 23
Ring of Brodgar, *59*
Roast fowl, 29, 73
Roman Catholic Church, 9,
23, 31
Rome, Ancient, 8-9, 14, 15,
27
Rowan, 27
Royal British Arms, *9*

S

St. Andrew's Cross, *9*
St. Magnus Cathedral, *25*
Santa Claus, 17, 25, 27
Saturnalia, 14, 15
Scots (ancient people), 9
Shetland Islands, 40, 54-63

Shinty, 53
Shortbread, 29, 30, 33, 38,
52
Sigurd, 63
Singin' E'en, 37
Skeklers, 40
Solstice, Winter, 12, 17, 19
Songs. *See also* Caroling
Hogmanay, 34, 37, 38,
41, 71-72
Up-Helly-A', 54, 57
Sowens, 30
Sports, 50-51, 53, 60-63
Standing stones, 60
Steak and kidney pie, 74
Stirling, 37-38, 45, 49, 51
Stonehaven, 15, 19
Stromness, 60
Sun, 60
winter solstice, 12, 17, 19
worship of, 12-14
Sun cakes, 30

T

Thigging, 52
Toasts, 10, 32
Trows, 59
Tusker, 62
Twelfth Night, 22, 64
Twelfth Night Cake. *See* Black
bun

U

Uphalieday, 64
Up-Helly-A', 54-58, 64
Uppies, 61-63

V

Venison stew, 75
Victorian age, 24
Vikings, 12, 14-17, 60
boat-burning tradition, 48,
54-58

W

Woden, 17, 27
Women's games, 62
Worship, 31

Y

Yule, 14-15, 21-24, 56-59. *See
also* Christmas
Yule, Margaret, 62

ACKNOWLEDGMENTS

Cover   © Dennis Hardley;
       © Angela Hampton, Travel Ink

2   © Dennis Hardley

5   © Paul Tomkins,
    Scottish Viewpoint

6   © Spectrum Colour Library

11   Mary Evans Picture Library

13   © Dennis Hardley

14   Mary Evans Picture Library

15   © Art Explosion

17   © Corbis

18   © Marjory Stephens

20   © Paul Tomkins,
    Scottish Viewpoint

22   Mary Evans Picture Library

25   © D. Houghton,
    Trip Photo Library

26-27   © Andreas von Einsiedel

28   © Anthony Blake Photo
    Library

29   © Andreas von Einsiedel

30   © The Tom Smith Group Ltd.,
    Norwich, England

31   © Tony Robins,
    Anthony Blake Photo Library

32   © H. Rogers, Trip Photo Library

35   Mary Evans Picture Library

36-37   © Alex Gillespie,
    Edinburgh Photographic
    Library

39   Mary Evans Picture Library

41   © PhotoDisc. Inc.

43   © Dennis Hardley

44   © Gary Doak,
    Scottish Viewpoint

47   © Marius Alexander,
    Scottish Viewpoint

48-49   © Gary Doak,
    Scottish Viewpoint

50   © Dennis Hardley

51   © Marius Alexander,
    Scottish Viewpoint

53   © Gordon Lennox

55-56   © Charles Tait

59   © D. Houghton,
    Trip Photo Library

60   © Richard Welsby;
    © Charles Tait

61   © Charles Tait

63   World Book photo by
    Dale DeBolt*

64   © Graham Kirk,
    Anthony Blake Photo Library

Craft Illustrations: Eileen Mueller Neill
and Kimberly Neill*

Recipe Cards: World Book photos by
Dale DeBolt*

Advent Calendar: Mary Evans
Picture Library

Advent Calendar Illustrations:
Eileen Mueller Neill*

All entries marked with an asterisk (*)
denote illustrations created exclusively
for World Book, Inc.